Turn Back The Clock

Lotta Vokes

A collection of stories written by nineteen neighbours and friends, yet another amusing device to throttle the boredom of the Covid lockdown of 2021

Lotta Vokes

Dublin. September 2021

Lotta Vokes

Scriptores

Bridget Aylmer

Chris Struelens

Dorothea McDowell

Patricia Storey

Alan, Grainger

Derek Phillips

Eleanor Bourke

Jillian Godsil

Killian O'Boyle

Maureen Grainger

Mike McDonnell

Susie Knight

Will Durston

Mary Cait Hermon

Micheal MacSuibhne

Miss Terrigest

Verell Booth

Pat Mullan

Natalie Cox

INDEX

Lotta Vokes

Seaside holidays, a Washing Machine, Roast Pork, and a Grandfather Clock.

by

Alan Grainger

When I wasn't at primary school, I spent most of my time with my cousin David. We were around five or six at the time and lived a few houses from each other on the same road. We lit bonfires in each other's gardens, sent smoke signals to Indian encampments, went on raiding parties to steal rhubarb, which we ate raw after dipping the ends in sugar. And we poked the tar from between the blue glasslike slag cobbles with which the road was surfaced, melted it in a tin lid over a candle, and turned it into catapult ammunition. We swapped cigarette cards and foreign stamps, played marbles, fished the beck for newts and sticklebacks, and generally had a good time.

The only person we'd permit to enter our world was David's aged Great Aunt Selina, a retired Post Mistress who lived with them, the only woman I'd ever seen wearing trousers. She'd bang on the window with her bony knuckles, beckoning us up to her room where she'd dole out bull's eyes, striped humbugs, banana split, treacle toffee, and candied violets (which smelled the same as my mother's underwear drawer).

David's brother, Colin, a year or two older than us, introduced me to carlings, black peas which, on Carling Sunday, people cooked into a brown porridge-like mess and ate as a thankful reminder of the hundreds who'd been saved from starvation when a cargo of carlings was washed ashore, following a shipwreck back in seventeen hundred and odd. We cooked them in an old tobacco tin on a bonfire and they tasted delicious.

He also eventually succeeded in convincing me that there were dead people's bodies inside the wooden boxes covered in flowers we'd see in the glass windowed back of the long black cars that frequently passed down our road. I wasn't so sure when he told me those same people were going to be buried in the ground ... how could that be?

I've many memories of that period of my life, but the best of them all, easily, were the days on which we played the new and sensational American board game everyone wanted and David had; Monopoly. At seven and six it was beyond most people but David's dad, my Uncle Harry, was rich ... he had a car.

Not that life was all play. I must tell you about 'The All American Washing Machine' for example. We got it in 1933 to help my mother cope with the household's laundering. To have such a machine in those days was rare, even if it *was* only 'boy' powered. Ours lasted the best part of forty years and was probably the most cost-effective domestic appliance my parents ever bought. I was about five or six when we got it, and I immediately insisted on being the motive force.

I can see myself now on washing mornings, standing in a steam filled shed we called 'The Washhouse' at the end of our garden waiting for my mother.

I'd be all 'ready to go', with my hand reaching towards the machine, a contraption taller than I was, all wood and cast iron, and fitted with a whacking great fly wheel that ensured the even application of my power to the gears and rollers.

And I can remember the thoughts which used to come into my head as my mother loaded the clothes into the cage, battened down the lid, and nodded the signal for me to start delivering momentum to get the process under way. I'd nod back and, tightening my puny muscles, throw my full weight against the handle. Gradually the machine's inertia would be overcome, slowly the revolutions would begin to build and, next thing, our clothes and sheets would be whizzing round in hot soapy suds.

Engulfed by the distinctive smell of 'washing', I'd pull even harder, lean into my task more enthusiastically to generate even greater speed to the imprisoned clothes.

Not that I'd see it like that. No, I'd be miles away in a world of my own. The flywheel wouldn't be part of our washing machine at all; it'd be a key component of the Queen Mary's engine, powering her through the Atlantic's waves to New York. The faster I turned, the faster would go the ship. Obvious.

We could beat the Normandie if we tried hard enough; we might even re-gain the Blue Ribband, awarded to the fasted liner to cross the Atlantic.

I'd be gasping for breath at that stage, and everything would be flying round: cage full of clothes, flywheel, handle ...me almost! ... And then ... panic ... the machine's momentum has taken over and *it's* driving *me*, what'll I do? I daren't let go or she'll yell at me. I did once; I let go the handle and it whipped round and cracked the back of my hand and made me cry. I didn't get much sympathy from my mother though … 'It's not a toy Alan,' she said, 'how many times have I told you?'

***

Our holidays back then, in the mid-thirties, were spent at Whitby, a north Yorkshire fishing port and seaside resort, and they were invariably preceded by the exciting ritual of 'packing the trunk'.

In those days if you had no car, and since my father left BP and lost his six cylinder Hotchkiss powered Bull Nosed Morris, we didn't have one; you went on holiday by train. And train meant lugging heavy suitcases, unless you did as we did, and packed all your things into a cabin trunk and 'sent it on ahead'.

Our trunk was large; a good three feet long, two feet wide, and as high. It was made of thick plywood covered with heavy green canvas strengthened by timber bands and brass corners. The formidable lock was of brass too, and it was doubly secured by hefty straps. The top was domed, and there was a leather carrying handle at each end for, when it was full, it took two men to carry it. It was a serious piece of luggage, one befitted to the important service it provided each summer.

For several days before it was due to be collected by the railway company's van, my mother would bustle about, washing and ironing the clothes we'd need, and then piling them on the spare room bed ready for packing, a task she always left to the last minute 'in case the weather changed'.

Once our clothes had been put into the main body of the trunk, other essential stuff like tennis rackets, box kites, beach toys, metal buckets and wooden spades, carefully saved from previous years, would be crammed into the tray sitting across the top and secured in position with teddy bears, dolls, rubber bouncing balls and wellington boots. Finally, the lid would be closed and locked before tightening the straps and attaching the labels. The excitement engendered by this thrilling ritual year after year, was kept on the boil by a daily countdown to departure day. It was like an advent calendar, sans chocolates!

We stayed at Highcliffe (or was it Eastcliffe?); a tall red brick four storied boarding house just off the sea front. I usually had a room at the very top, one with a little dormer window from which, if I stood on tiptoe, I could see a good stretch of the beach, the sea, and the ice cream van parked on the promenade. On a highly decorative board over its drop- down counter was emblazoned the name of the owner ... Alessandro Pacitto. What a name, what a man and what amazing ice creams he made. His penny cornets were as big as today's Whippys.

Those pre-war seaside holidays were wonderful. All day long on the beach, usually in the company of other children who'd been tempted to join the CSSM (Christian Sunday School Mission) by the games programme it provided.

Run by a group of university students, the CSSM kept us all well occupied. On the beach, first thing each morning, we'd dig out the sand to form seating benches on which we'd place wooden planks. For the next half hour, we'd sit there singing popular hymns, accompanied by one of the students on a portable harmonium. The rest of the day would be left for fun. There'd be treasure and scavenger hunts, Beach Ball, French Cricket, Rounders, Football, and Sand Castle building, plus all the usual games like Tig and Bung the Barrel, as well as supervised swimming trips when the tide was right.

Our parents sat on the striped canvas seats of wooden deck chairs in front of the beach hut they'd rented, telling themselves how lucky they were. The huts served to change in, to store deck chairs and beach paraphernalia in, and, on a noisy primus stove, to make tea. Unfortunately, we also had to use it frequently to shelter from showers driving in from the sea. I can clearly remember the smell of wet clothes and burning paraffin as we huddled together waiting for the kettle to boil and the rain to cease. Mind you, on a sunny day, Whitby is the business.

We often went to Pierrot or Seaside Concert

Party shows, or fished off the harbour wall. On one amusing but painful day, my father, not the best to cast a line, triple-hooked himself through the back of his thigh and had to be bloodily cut free by the man fishing next to us. He carried out the crude 'hook-ectomy' with his penknife.

We also used to look for Lobby Lud, a man who worked for the Westminster Gazette, and who roamed from one seaside town to the next, carrying a copy of that day's edition in his hand. No one knew where he was likely to turn up but, armed with a current copy oneself, a successful challenge as to his identity could win you a prize of ten pounds. 'You are Lobby Lud and I claim the ten pound prize.' I'd say to anyone holding a paper I spotted, but I never managed to ask the right man. It was a popular game which produced much amusement as people all over the country made a bee-line for anyone carrying a newspaper. I can't imagine how many Lobby Luds there must have been spread around the country to keep the fun going and the Gazette's sales climbing, quite a few!

I've been back to Whitby twice in recent years - it's hardly changed at all except for the ice cream van opposite Highcliffe, it's vanished. Not that Alessandro Pacitto has gone out of business, no … he's just gone out of ice cream vans, and moved into a swanky new all chrome and mirror-glass premises in the new shopping centre down by the harbour.

During those 'between the wars' years, and before we moved to London in 1936, I suppose one of my most enduring memories is that of Sunday lunch … always a big family gathering … one which invariably took place at my mother's parent's house, Harrow Lodge. There were never less than a dozen of us at the table.

The ladies generally congregated in the kitchen as they arrived and, while there, as they prepared the food, they'd pass my baby sister Susan from one lap to the next and swap scandal. Great

Aunt Annie's high-pitched giggle which punctuated every remark, and which never seemed to stop, always appeared to be loud enough to filter through to annoy the men, sitting in the drawing room, smoking and debating matters of the day.

I'd wander backwards and forwards between my elders who, apart from Grandpa, paid me scant attention. If he saw a look of boredom on my face, he'd take my hand and lead me upstairs to his consulting room, where he kept a few toys for our personal entertainment.

The minute we were through the door we'd drop to our knees and set up the rails of the Hornby train set he had there expressly for me. Or we'd sit at the table and play Fox and Geese on a round polished mahogany board with some old glass marbles he'd brought back from when he worked in Germany. Quite often he'd take out a burnished brass working model of a steam engine, light up the methylated spirit burner, boil up the water, and then slowly, slowly, as the pressure built, we'd watch the piston began to reciprocate in the open sided sleeve. Its movement drove a pulley wheel from which, in the real thing, power to run a mighty machine could be taken off, but Grandpa and I used it to drive a windmill we'd built out of gold painted Meccano.

He was a small man, Grandpa, as were all the Lawsons, and I only remember him in a grey suit reeking of cigar smoke. Dangling from his waistcoat pocket and draped across his stomach, he usually had a heavy gold chain at the end of which was a fob-watch which chimed. Those intimate moments with him made a great impression on me, leaving me with little difficulty in recalling his appearance, and his scent, though he died eighty-eight years ago.

The meal, when we eventually sat down to it, would be huge; two joints usually, one of which would always be pork, clad with a crust of slightly burned and bubbling crackling. As he carved me a slice from the outside and passed the plate to my mother to add vegetables, he'd wink at me. 'Give him plenty Mary,' he'd say, 'he's a growing boy.' I'm convinced, looking back on it now, that by ensuring I got a hefty serving each Sunday, he was unconsciously laying the foundation of my present fourteen and a half stone.

There'd be puddings to follow, often cream topped trifle which I loved, or tinned apricots which I didn't. After lunch Grandpa'd fetch the Wedgewood Stilton dish from the sideboard, somehow managing to do it with a style he normally reserved to welcome important guests. Then he'd lift the lid, and bend to sniff and savour the wheel of napkin wrapped cheese. I disliked the stink of Stilton then but I've changed since; now I love its inviting aroma, it's my favourite cheese - a noble beast - and best fitted to end a meal not interrupt it, as do sophisticates and Frenchmen.

Sometimes I'd stay overnight at Harrow Lodge, a slightly scary experience. On those occasions I'd sleep in a high feather bed smelling of camphor, in a room over the front hall. On the top of the tallboy chest looking down at me with a terrifying degree of menace, I recall there being a white china figure of a large polar bear. It seemed so real in the semi darkness I'd hide my head beneath the bedclothes clutching the 'stone' hot water bottle in a knitted jacket my grandmother always put in for me.

The principal recollection I have of that house though, apart from Grandpa's cigar smell, Sunday lunches, the steam engine, the polar bear, and his tales of his perilous race to The Klondike in 1898 in search of gold, is that of the Grandfather clock which stood in the hall. It's in *my* hall now and, when I hear it chiming in the night, I'm immediately taken back to my childhood, my Grandparents, and my fading memories of their tall dark house.

Bears in Belgium.

in Wezembeek-Oppem around 1956,

by

Chris Struelens.

The first years of my life we lived in my grandmother's house on my father' side. My grandmother was a widow and the house was too big for her alone. As you walked from the street to the house there was a path leading to the front door, it continued left and right from the house to the backyard. A few steps led up to the front door. Behind the door you came to the stairs and a corridor that ran through to the back. There was a left side of the stairs and a right side. My grandmother lived on the left - three consecutive rooms. We lived on the right and also had three rooms. Oddly enough, it was reversed upstairs - with us on the left and her on the right. Our side had my father's small sitting room cum study, that contained a sofa, bookcases and an armchair. Then there was also a living-room-kitchen and a utility room. There was no central heating, which came later.

When we were little, we were washed in a washing tub in front of the stove. My brother was 13 months older than me. We also had a play cellar downstairs.

Behind the house was a lawn where we played, after that came my grandmother's vegetable garden, off limits to us. And then there was the orchard and the chicken run.

After our wash on Saturday evening, my mother prepared the chicken soup for Sunday. On Saturdays we were allowed to stay up longer, with our wet hair, and it was when we were sitting in front of the desk that the arguments began.

My brother had a Teddy bear you see; a thick furred fine soft bear. The Teddy I had was not that big and not that fluffy. I had been jealous of my brother's Teddy for a long time. And, as happened so often, I had taken his Teddy away and was sitting, holding it like a trophy … on the sofa.

My brother claimed rightful possession of his bear, and so the conflict started. I clutched it in a stranglehold in my arms. My brother couldn't bear it any longer and gave me a good slap. Of course, I slapped him back, and moments later we were both crying.

My father left us alone for a while, and then took both my bear and my brother's and placed them high and dry on top of his bookshelf. My bear looked at me sweetly from up there.

My brother backed off and I saw my chance. Like a monkey, I started to climb the bookshelf with my goal in sight. The bookshelf started to wobble, my father jumped forward and grabbed me by my pyjamas just before the shelf with all its contents fell.

Both bears lay on the ground and, as I was not willing to give up, I made one last attempt to grab the bear in question. The rest of the evening I sat on the seat, punished, and was not allowed to move a finger. My brother sat on the other side of the seat with his soft fluffy bear in his arms.

Now, so many years later, I know that my bear had been a much more expensive one and was still in good condition, whereas my brother's bear's fluff had disappeared over the years.

What I still remember though, even more than the bears, is the smell of chicken soup, our wet hair, and my grandmother joining us every Saturday night. They were happy moments.

In 1960 my parents built a new house farther down the street. The house had every comfort. I had my own bedroom, there was a bathroom and central heating, a brand-new kitchen and large garden, all the trimmings. But for me, nothing could ever compare to my grandmother's house just three houses down the street.

The Pretty Maiden

by

Verell Booth

With her short skirts, her beret perched on one side of her head, her hair artfully arranged in a kiss curl on the other side of her face, she was to their six and eight year old eyes someone outside their normal experience, quite unlike the other women who inhabited their world. They thought she was beautiful. They didn't realize that the rosy cheeks and cupid's bow mouth owed nothing to nature; in the mid nineteen twenties makeup was unknown to them.

She lived in a flat further up the terrace, in a house which unusually at that time was divided in two, with separate hall doors. The terrace had its own driveway and gardens bounded by iron railings, so the children were safe to play out of doors.

The other neighbours were mostly elderly. Or so they seemed to the children, and did not pay much attention to them, but the "Pretty Maiden" as they had christened her, always stopped to talk to them when she was passing by, asking them about whatever game they were playing, and sometimes giving them sweets. In those innocent days they were given no warnings against taking sweets from strangers, and any way, even if they had, they did not look upon her as a stranger.

The Pretty Maiden's name was Josie, and she lived with her father, she said.

She invited the children into her flat one afternoon, and fascinated but vaguely uneasy, they followed her up the stairs and into a room which was like one of the rooms in their own house that had been cut in half. "Daddy," she said to a man sitting in an arm chair, reading a newspaper, "here are some visitors for you."

The man didn't look very pleased to see them, and grunted crossly in reply to their polite "How do you do?" which they had heard grown-ups say in greeting.

"Where do they come from?" he asked Josie.

"They live down the terrace, I told you about them."

"I thought I said you were not to get familiar with the people around here."

"But sure, they're only kids, what harm can they do?"

"Kids talk, don't they?"

"Go into the kitchen children, just through there," she said, indicating a door, "I'll be in there in a minute and I'll get you some lemonade."

She closed the door behind them, and they could hear the man shouting at her. They looked at each other in dismay. Imagine any Daddy talking like that! They felt very frightened, and wanted to run home, only there was no way out except through the room they had just left.

The door opened and Josie came in.

"Now, what about some lemonade?" She took a bottle from a cupboard, and they saw it was fizzy lemonade. The little boy said "Yes please," but his sister, giving him a push, whispered fiercely, "You know Mummy doesn't let us have it!", and thanking her, said "I think we'd better go now."

The woman looked sadly at them, and didn't try to persuade them to stay. Making themselves as small as possible they crept through the room, ran down the stairs and out through the hall door.

The next time they saw Josie they felt a little awkward, they didn't know if she would be angry with them for running away like that, but she didn't seem to mind, and talked to them just as she usually did.

Sometimes Josie was with the man she called 'Daddy'. When she was, the children used to pretend they hadn't seen them and turned away from them until they had passed.

Then, one day, they saw him by himself, leaving the terrace, carrying a suitcase. About a week later another man went into the flat, but he only stayed a short while. This happened several times, only there seemed to be different men going in. They puzzled over this ... who could they be? And why had her Daddy gone away? They made up stories about him. Perhaps he was a sailor, maybe he had been shipwrecked and, although they knew it was wrong, they hoped he would be, because he had been so horrid to the Pretty Maiden.

They were speculating about this one evening, after tea, when their mother overheard them.

"Who are you talking about?" She asked.

"The Pretty Maiden - she lives in the flat."

"You mean the flat at number eight?"

"Yes, we went in one day, but her daddy was horrid to her so we came away."

Their mother frowned. "You shouldn't have

gone there without asking me. I think I'd rather you didn't speak to her anymore."

"But why? She's nice; she's our friend."

"No, children, you must do as I say. You'll understand when you're older."

They were very upset by this, but obeyed their mother and just said "Hello" and "Goodbye" when they saw their friend, and did not enter into conversation with her.

She said once "Are you not talking to me these days?"

Red with embarrassment, and not looking at her, the older child mumbled "We're not allowed… and "Mummy told us …"

"Oh, I see," the Pretty Maiden said, "well I'm sorry about that, but you must do what your mother tells you." Her voice sounded funny and she walked away slowly.

The children felt sad, and their game lost its interest for them. They went home and were very quiet for the rest of the day, pondering on the strangeness of grownups.

A few days later, while they were playing in the garden there was a sudden flurry of activity down the terrace. Several Civic Guards converged upon the flat at number eight and a crowd quickly gathered. Full of curiosity the children ran along to see what was happening. They arrived just in time to see the man they knew as Daddy being led away by the Guards. Edging in between the onlookers the children asked a man "Where's the Pretty Maiden?"

"What do you mean, who are you talking about?"

"The lady who lives there, the Pretty Maiden."

"Huh … Not after he finished with her…"

"For God's sake man, not in front of the kids!" interrupted a woman, "Off home with you children, you shouldn't be here."

Reluctantly they moved away, but not before they heard the man say, "God rest her, she's no Pretty Maiden now."

Wexford: A country Retreat.

by

Killian O'Boyle

My mother and I share a darkened bedroom. In the morning I watch earwigs scuttle across a linoleumed land brandishing battle ready nippers to fend off foes - ants maybe as they're plentiful too.

After breakfast I wander outside where the late summer warms my freckling face and sit atop a sun trapped grassy seat nestled under a ferned hedge. Beyond the hedge a tightly manicured laneway with a trim green centre wheedles and meanders past another holiday house or two and on to the sea via gilded wheat fields. The sound of a push mower as it gently scythes the grass catches my attention. My grandfather is at work. My Nana, a graceful grey-haired woman, tenderly maintains her vegetable plot. The runner beans have wrapped themselves around the bamboo sticks supporting them as she brings me some freshly picked peas that awaken a sweet lasting taste - a forever memory. We bask in the morning sun as the soothing sea glints beyond.

Later Nana works away in the kitchen. Mum helps her prepare the main meal of the day. Home cooked aromas billow out from behind the curtained kitchenette. I set the table as best I can. Warmed brown bread melts butter into a golden gorgeousness. The garden grown ingredients ensure a perfectly complementing soup. New potatoes steam the room and blackberries, picked from the brambled hedge, make a sumptuous end of summer tart.

After dinner we head outside past the bunkered shed, standing cold and useful, roughly roofed with corrugated Perspex. A bronzed, bald and bespectacled crown bends forward tidying stones spilled from the pebble crowded drive. Grandad is the fastidious keeper of a humble yet perfect holiday home. Soon the autumn will come and the house and garden will stand together and endure the winter before the next spring draws the swallows away from the unbearable North African summer heat.

I peer through the hedge into the field beyond. At the far end sits an alabaster white painted caravan. Our caravan. A caravan we take on our summer holidays. It is our field; my parents' field. And soon we too will build a summer house. A house of our own. A house for the five of us for now we are still only three. Number four is already growing in my mother's tummy. The future is coming.

Ten years later.....

My grandparents have left their idyl and my parents and two younger sisters are reviewing the building work on our own summer home. The now creamy coloured caravan has grown a green skin having lived under a leylandii tree for several years. The roof light leaks and its years of faithful service are coming to an end. It has served this family well. We walk around the foundations of our future summer holidays. The bedrooms seem tiny. As yet unbuilt, they are marked out. There's excitement in the air. After it's 'shell and cored' and the money spent, the painting and fitting has to be done. The used white goods will be fine here. The living/dining/kitchen room is split by a semi circled wall whitewashed and topped with a homemade yellow tiled work top. My father's handy abilities make the impossible probable. High wooden stools tucked beneath the kitchen counter … Americana chic that Dublin south side bourgeoisie have yet to make de rigueur!

Our childhood was full of Wexford working. Painting, cleaning, making, fixing. In the early years the house was let out to pay the bills. There were no cheap flights. Ryanair was a financial basket case. Holidays in Ireland were the norm for the masses and cash payment was king. On many a summer Saturday

Dad and I would travel to Wexford from Dublin in the morning, check-out the tenants from the week before, clean the house, make the beds and check-in next week's family. The day Dad got a fifty-pound note was memorable. So was the rushing to Wexford to buy replacement mattresses after one sneaky family managed to pee in every mattress. That put paid to the value of the fifty pounds!

But, after a couple of summers of 'sweating the asset', renting it out didn't seem so necessary. Three-month summer holidays in Wexford became the norm. Other kids went to mobile home parks in Brittas Bay or Courtown but we always felt that no wolf, wind or rain would blow our house down and that bumping into all the eejits in a caravan park would be painful at best. So, we enjoyed our less well-known summer home down the secret laneway with the still working water pump where the track met the road.

The beach was magic. We walked to it through the golden wheat fields using the fisherman's right of way while avoiding the grumpy farmer who didn't like us cutting through his land. But we were great at dodging him and the threat of a chase kept us on our toes. The white sandy beach stretched for miles each way unknown to many until the silver screen broadcast it to millions of people years later in two Hollywood blockbusters. But for us it will always be Tayto crisps and cheese sandwiches in the dunes, long walks, warm summer waters and moonlit nights.

Back in the house wood burned in the open fire roasting our little child faces as we watched Welsh television beamed down the rickety aerial attached to the chimney. The televisual feast of the summer was none other than the Rose of Tralee where we'd rate all the lovely girls and giggle at the mental cases flown in from all parts of America. Board games were a main staple of summer fun, especially when the Irish summer rained down. (Hurricane Charlie lashed the house in 1986 before climate change was a thing). Boggle, Monopoly,

Scrabble, card games and the king of 1980s board games, the one and only Trivial Pursuit, kept us enlightened and educated in all things inconsequential before Tim Berners Lee's internet ruined the art of blagging our way through questions; before Google knew it all!

As we got older our friends came to stay and the sealed family unit got invaded by boys and girls who also had great fun. But Wexford was primarily about our family. A family retreat. A quiet place, with a million bright stars overhead on summer nights. In the fields and villages around locals still lived, loved and had big families. 10 kids plus in the houses nearby wasn't unheard of. Development and progress were slow. Going to mass was different. It seemed brighter and more engaging than the Dublin experience. The priest would talk about his excitement at seeing Spring's first swallow at Easter mass with its forecast of better summer weather to come. The sounds and smells from the farm next door were exciting for little kids. The convent down the road was a retreat for aging nuns. And there were gaggles of them. You can spot nuns not just by their habits but also by their driving. It's awful. As my father often said it looked like they were praying the car would get them where they needed to go rather than using the gears. The 1980s economic stagnation was a good thing in many ways. It held back time, economic growth and 'progress'. Thatched cottages were common and beautiful to walk past on a quiet road. The people were pleasant and the sounds were softer.

The swallows still come and go and the house is now bigger. A new generation is enjoying the laneway, the blackberries, the summer evenings and the beautiful beach. Soon enough perhaps a 5th generation will gurgle and dribble their first summer holiday there too.

The Yellow and Purple House

by

Susie Knight

My grandparents ran away to start a new life in Brooklyn, New York in the late 1920s. They pretended that they were married, but they were not, because my grandfather was already married and had a wife and three children back in London! Divorce in England was very difficult at that time and was only granted on the grounds of adultery. However, if the adulterer could not be found or was abroad for seven years, a marriage could be annulled. This is probably why they went to America. They either thought that they could make a new life there or that they could return to England after seven years in order to marry.

The first few years in New York must have been very exciting. High rise buildings like The Empire State Building which was, at the time, the tallest building in the world, Times Square, trips to Staten Island and evenings at the Speakeasy or at a Jazz Club!

The 1920s in the USA was also a time of racism and fear of other peoples' cultures. Many people were travelling to America to seek their fortunes, and to start a new life. New York was a melting pot of peoples from across the world.

However, black Americans were still enslaved and segregated from white people. Black people were considered to be inferior to their white compatriots and were discriminated against in many unpleasant ways. I remember my grandmother telling me that there were drinking fountains for black people and fountains for white people. They were labelled 'Blacks Only' or 'Whites Only', and she said that you should never drink from them because they were dirty, and you could catch diseases and die! This image had such an impact on me, that I have never been able to drink from a water fountain from that day to this!

The early twenties in New York would have been exhilarating and my Grandparents must have thought they had found the land of milk and honey. There are photographs of them having parties on the beach with friends or dressed up outside restaurants. However, the early 1930's were very different. The Wall Street Crash had happened in 1929 and America was no longer the vibrant place it had been. People were out of work and immigrants were no longer wanted. My grandparents found that they could not survive; having lost their jobs. This meant that they had to return to England, which had not been part of their plan.

When they got back, they had to find work and somewhere to live. But England was also in a depression, so work was hard to find and by then they had a tiny baby.

They eventually found a small house in East London and settled there. The house was typical of the time. It had no heating, just one small fire grate in the sitting room. However, it was a start.

During the next five years, they had another two children but then 1939 saw the beginning of World War Two. My grandfather built an air raid shelter in the garden, as they were living in East London where much of the bombing was focused. It must have been terrifying! I remember my grandmother telling me the story of the night that she was cooking sausages for tea, when the air raid siren sounded. They all rushed out to the shelter, my grandfather bringing up the rear with the pan of sausages. A bomb exploded in the next street and he was blown into the shelter, and the sausages flew everywhere! However, they all survived and, as if to celebrate, my grandmother and grandfather married in 1944. How they managed this I am not quite sure, as he was still married to his first wife.

Their three children grew up and the eldest, my mother, was married in the early 1950's. However, things did not work out and she left her husband and returned to live with her parents. By this time, she had me, as a baby. My mum had to work and so I was looked after by my grandmother or "Nan" as I called her!

I have such vivid memories of the house and the things in it. There were unusual items that they had bought back from America, like a cigarette making machine on a black lacquered stand and a wooden water buffalo with a baby that slotted into the mother.

Eventually, I went to the local school. East London was changing, and different kinds of people were coming to live in the locality. An Indian family called Singh moved into a house two roads up from ours, and they had a daughter called Jasmin, who was in my class at school. There was a lot of gossip about the Singh family. Most of the houses in our streets were painted dark green or brown and cream, but the Singh's painted their house purple and yellow. People were outraged! I thought it was lovely.

I became quite friendly with Jasmin and we used to walk to school together. My grandmother told me that under no circumstances was I to go into her house.

I asked her why?

She said that there would be lots of men lying on top of each other on the floor, sweating. I was somewhat puzzled by this thought. Why would there be lots of men? Why would they be sweating?

Jasmin had to deal with other children calling her names. All children had to deal with name calling to some degree. Four Eyes, Fatty, Big Ears etc. Nevertheless, some of the names that they shouted at

Jasmine seemed very unkind. The other girls did not want to play with her. I understood this because I had trouble with friends too, I didn't have a dad you see! So, I made friends with her and we got on very well.

Jasmin asked me if I would like to go to her house for tea. I really wanted to go; I wanted to see what the Yellow and Purple house was like. So, without telling my Nan, I went.

I carefully stepped through the yellow front door and looked around, but I couldn't see any sweating men. In fact, it looked just like my house, but with more colour. The sitting room had a sofa and a chair, and it was full of bright colours, drifty material and big cushions.

Jasmin's mum was wearing a sari, she spoke good English and she brought us some drinks and biscuits. We ate them and then Jasmin asked me if I would like to play in her room. We went up the stairs. I was nervous about going upstairs because 'the sweating men' might be up there! I went up slowly, listening for the breathing of the sweating men. But there was nothing to see. I went into Jasmin's room; it was an ordinary bedroom. We played with her things. I was fascinated by her dolls. They had dark skin and shiny black hair like her family. I had never seen brown dolls before.

After a while I said it was time for me to go home. I went down the stairs and said thankyou and goodbye to her mum. I walked home and wondered about the sweating men! Where were they? Maybe they were in the loft?

I returned home and my Nan asked me where I had been.

I said, "Oh I've been to Jasmin's house".

There was a silence, and then my Nan asked "What was it like? I thought I told you not to go there!"

"Oh, it was lovely, very colourful! She has brown dolls, but there were no sweating men!"

She did not say any more.

In later years, I was responsible for promoting

equality and diversity in my work. I often used this story as an example of how prejudice can be created and imagined from images and ideas in stories and pictures, and then unfairly applied to groups of people.

I think my Nan's prejudice came from having seen pictures of slaves in the bottom of slave ships, sweating due to overcrowding, starvation, cruelty and over work. I think her experience of segregation in America, plus her memory of the slave pictures had created a fear in her of people who were not like her.

She was not a cruel or an unkind person, she was however, prejudiced!

If you see a Fairy Ring

by

Dorothea McDowell

Mid-Summer Day August 1956, aged 10, on
my Aunt Lizzie's farm in Co. Cavan 100
miles north of Dublin.

If you see a fairy ring
In a field of grass,
Very lightly step around,
Tiptoe as you pass;
Last night fairies frolicked there,
And they're sleeping somewhere near.
If you see a tiny fairy
Lying fast asleep,
Shut your eyes and run away,
Do not stay or peep;
And be sure you never tell,
Or you'll break a fairy spell.

William Shakespeare

Shannon Pot: Cuilcagh Mountain – is the source of the River Shannon. According to legend, it is named after **Sionnan,** who was the granddaughter of **Manannanmac Lir, the God of the Sea.** She came to this spot to eat the forbidden fruit of the Tree of Knowledge, which was planted by the Druids. As she began to eat it, the waters of the pool sprang up and overwhelmed her. She was drawn down into the pool and its water began to flow over the land, forming the River Shannon.

An insight into my childhood points to my father's sister, Elizabeth, who lived on an idyllic farm with glorious flowers in front of her cottage; dahlias in profusion surrounded by brilliant white outbuildings and only a few miles from her original home. She was an eccentric woman who had an incredible awareness of the *real* world of nature - of milking thirty cows and running her fifty acres economically enough to give her a comfortable lifestyle. She was *otherworldly* in-tune with the *fairy* realm too. I looked forward to those idyllic summers in that setting, one hundred miles due north of Dublin, amongst the Cavan lakes and drumlins. For there I experienced a world of magic during the summer holidays of 1951-1957 when I was between five and twelve; the seven year period that can be so significant to a child which, I suppose, is why they keep cropping up in my autobiography.

Thrilled when crowded into a taxi to take us away from the strict confines of our lives in the city, my sisters, Maura and Kate and I, were encouraged to identify car registration numbers and count cat's eyes to keep us quiet. Father conducted proceedings from the passenger seat as, due to his asthmatic condition, he was unable to drive. The local taxi man being on call for all our business and pleasure outings. On those special days at Aunt Lizzie's though, I'd awake as usual at dawn and scramble into my working clothes, ready for a day that would continue with one activity after another. My tasks were to hand feed two baby calves, saw tree branches into pieces of wood for the open fire, make ropes to tie down the haycocks, and bring tea to the farmhand, Galligan, in the long meadow.

Before all this happened though, at around eight in the morning, I'd run through one field after another looking for *Willie*, the shire horse; to coax him to the hedgerow where I'd climb up on his wide back and ride him to the yard, where he'd be harnessed into the cart to carry out his first duty of the day ... delivering milk churns to the local creamery. In the afternoon, Willie would be harnessed to the plough, and he'd walk up and down the field creating furrows in the upturned soil in which the seed was spread. Later, in the autumn, wheat that had magically appeared would blow to and fro in the wind.

Harvesting starts when the leaves and stem turn yellow in colour and become fairly dry. It was in Willie's nature to be calm, a gentle animal and, to this day, I look back in wonder as to how he tolerated a young city girl putting on the bridle over his head, and fearlessly guiding him to the farmyard to commence his work routine.

In my dreamlike state, just after lunch, I'd wander into the *circular* field imagining the *little people* sleeping under the *fairy* tree or, on another occasion, perhaps if I was lucky, see them hanging out their clothes to dry. I lingered there, oblivious of time, lying out under the blazing sun, jerking back into reality as my thoughts came back making me wonder what I had to do next.

And then, in a flash of excitement, it would come to me, and I would gingerly run through the stubbled fields in my canvas shoes to the edge of the lake. There I'd gather the herd of cows and bring them back three hours before they were due to be milked. They'd create a furore in the gateway, expecting to be put in the byre at once. My aunt wondered out loud how the cows happened to be there as I hid behind a bush unseen by the human eye. She never ventured out until the sun set so, as soon as twilight came, at around 11.00 o'clock, she and I would enter into the night's entertainment, gingerly;

walking through the big meadow and bogland under the night's sky, sometimes starlit, oftentimes starless, looking out for a bog-hole in which I could have been lost in forever, while she told stories of elves working under the stars and moonlight to feed and clothe their families. We were on our way to a ceili in *Big Maggie's* picturesque cottage one night and I'd quizzed her on the magical life of the *wee folk*. 'Look,' I said, 'the tree is shaking, let's creep up and see them dancing.'

I can still hear my eccentric aunt's deep colloquial voice urging me on to our destination where a ceili was in full swing. 'Take care,' she'd say: 'they are cleverer than you and I, their psychic makes them wary of human danger. Look back, we can still see the oil lamp in our window, we will be late!'

My natural curiosity to experience the unknown had, for a short while, propelled my thinking back into the world of wonder.

I remember, I remember

By

Michael Alphonsus [Frank] McDonnell.

As Frank sat looking out over Smyrna Square having a cool Sweetwater 420. His focus turned to the Village Tavern across the square where a Guinness harp sign was displayed in the window. Next door was the corner Taqueria. A few doors away was a Sushi bar. It was an overcast day and it had just begun to rain. The scene brought back memories of his childhood in Ireland and his later extensive World travels to remote parts of the globe.

Frank grew up in the Northwest of Ireland, County Mayo. His earliest memories brought him back to about 1944-5, toward the end of World War two. Frank was the youngest of a family of nine, eight living siblings. There were five sisters, Mary, Annie, Philomena, Margaret, and Catherine. Four Brothers, Paddy, John, Leo, who died at age two and Frank the youngest. There was an age difference of 14 years between Frank and his oldest sibling, his sister, Mary.

He remembers the chilly winter nights around the flaming turf fire and the yellow glow cast by the paraffin oil lantern hanging on the wall. He recalls his father sitting close to the lantern, while he tried to read the local newspaper which came out once a week. Sometimes his parents would have to resort to candles as a light source, as Paraffin oil was rationed and not always available.

The local paper "The Western People" covered local news and topics of interest to the community. It also published, dates and times of sporting events around the area. Frank and his brothers would later be avid interested readers and participants in those events.

His play time with his father and siblings

involved playing around the house in a game that required one person to wear a blindfold and find a specific person. A simple game but one of great excitement for a young child. Frank's travel was limited only by his ability to walk or run wherever he wished, and his freedom was infinite. Frank was adventurous and inquisitive. The village had five residences, spaced on land holdings of 45 to 80 acres.

Frank's father was a transplant from a distant village, under the old land commission transplant scheme. He was an outsider in the village as the locals wanted the land for themselves. His father had given up two hundred acres of mostly bog land for forty-five acres of more arable land, a new house and two new barns. Also in the center of the land holding was a large derelict house, remnants of what was known locally as 'The Castle.' The move away from the old village where the family had lived for the past two hundred plus years, was dramatic and difficult. It is believed, Frank's great, great grandfather had moved there from Scotland to that remote place in early seventeen hundred. His gravestone only gives the year of passing, 1768.

Frank's father and mother moved into their new home in 1940. His father, Michael, and his wife, Bridget, had busy but simple lives. Times were tough, as they were for most people during the war.

Frank remembers the staple diet during those years was, Indian meal referred to as Gruel, a kind of a porridge. It came in large jute bags with American markings. Money was scarce and bartering among the local village people for certain items was common in those days, particularly for sugar and flour.

Frank's father had few friends in the community at first, except for John [Sonny] McKinley and John Sharp, both were Protestant families living in the adjacent village. There was one other Transplanted family, Joe O'Boyle, and his wife who was always known as Ann Traynor. An oddity, which Frank never understood; they had no children.

Frank's father would establish a close

friendship with the McKinley's and would visit the McKinley home frequently particularly during the winter months. Sometimes he would take Frank with him. Frank enjoyed his visits to the McKinley home. Sonny's wife Elizabeth had died young in 1934 and he had become a particularly good cook and baker. The McKinley home was close to John Sharp, who was a Batchelor. He would also be visiting. They would talk about local topics, notable events in the world as reported in the National newspaper and smoke their pipes. McKinley's had a large apple orchard and gooseberry patch. Sonny made delicious apple and gooseberry pies. Sonny would give Frank plenty of whatever vintage pie he had baked that day. He would also invite Frank and his brother John to help pick the gooseberries when ripe. He was generous and would give each of the children half a crown for a basket of gooseberries and of course all the gooseberries they could eat.

Frank's mother was an extraordinary industrious woman. She ran the home and had an endless list of projects and chores to keep her family busy. Frank was the only member of the family born in the new homestead and being the youngest got the easiest tasks. Those were bringing in turf for the fire, checking on the hens and ducks, and later responsible for the egg count for the traveling shop that would come by every two weeks on a Monday.

His first memory a trip outside his home was a visit to his aunt Katie. She was married to Jim Lynn of Shanvolahan a village back near where Frank's parents had lived. He was only about 3 years old but clearly remembers riding on the carrier of his mother's bicycle for twelve miles. When they arrived, they were greeted by the Lynn family and brought into the house - a large one for those times.

His Aunt Katie was an elegant lady with a unique voice and very gentle demeanor. She was dressed in a long black dress that reached her ankles. She wore a glittering green reflective broach and had golden hair tied back in a bun. She had a daughter, Pauline, his first cousin. She was kind and had a gentle smile. He felt her kindness as she was very friendly. She took his coat to hang it up. He was upset, as no one had ever taken his coat away before. He did not want her to take it, but the promise of some sweets solved the problem. He recalls her father Jim Lynn, who appeared incredibly old. A tall man with a grey beard. Frank still savours the memory of that pleasant visit and the sweets he got.

Back home he became acquainted with the neighbours. At the bottom of the road, was Spink Hill, about four hundred yards distance, where the Spellman's lived. There were two families living in nearby older thatched homes. The two houses were thatched with a local sedge, bordered, and scalloped with sally rods on the edges. They were attractive whitewashed homes in the old style with a livestock barn attached to each opposing end. A space of about twenty feet separated the two houses.

Thomas Spellman, who Frank would later learn was his God father, lived in the first house. His sister Mariah Dooher was Frank's God mother. She visited Thomas frequently. Mariah was the cook for the Harry Knox family estate, known as "The Greenwood big house." Frank would later enjoy her fine cooking in the form of sweet cakes for birthdays and other festive occasions. Thomas was married to Mary, and they had one son Tony. His wife was pregnant. She was the first pregnant woman Frank had ever seen.

Next door, William Spellman, a cousin of Thomas lived with his wife Ann, and they had seven daughters, all tall and strikingly beautiful. They were older. The youngest Patsy was seven years older than Frank.

The Next-door neighbours were the Cuffe's who were younger and had two sons and three daughters. The oldest was a boy named PJ, same age as Frank. Twin girls, Margaret & Patricia and a third daughter, Theresa and a young son, named Michael.

Frank's early memories were those of his immediate family and the village inhabitants which numbered thirty-one in 1947. He also remembers, the frequent visitors, from the old village of Corvoderra, and from the USA.

Frank remembers, one visitor from America in particular, who came to see his mother. It was in the Summer of 1947, she was a lovely lady, very tall and wore a blue suit and a large hat with a colourful feather. Her name was Delia. She was a friend of Frank's mother when they had worked together for the Parish Priest in Lahardane. Frank's mother was incredibly happy to see her old friend from so long ago. Delia had left to go to America as a young girl in 1912. She was 16 years old then, two years older than Frank's Mother. She had booked a passage on the ill-fated 'Titanic' and had survived. Several of her young friends from the village of Addergool, perished. Surely, she must have had some tales to tell having survived such a historic disaster. They spent the entire day visiting and having tea and Frank's Mother had cooked dinner. Frank tended to his chores of bringing water from the well, feeding the ducks and chickens and kept the fire well fuelled with turf while his mother and Delia talked all day. His Mother was sad when Delia left that summer evening at dusk. Delia would return to America, a place she said had "endless possibilities." At the time Frank did not know what all that meant? They would never meet her again.

Frank's next vivid memory was also in September ,1947 when the Davis family, neighbours from the   next village got a new wireless radio, in time for the All-Ireland final between Kerry and Cavan. It was all so exciting, as for the first and only time, the All Ireland, Gaelic Football final was played outside Ireland, at the Polo Grounds in New York. Frank and his two brothers were invited to listen to the broadcast. John Davis and his wife had five sons, Marty, Paul, Johnny, Paddy and Noel. They were similar in age to Billy and his two brothers. They also had two daughters, Philomena, and May. There were many people there and some had to stand in the roadside outside the old farmhouse. As the Radio announcer came on to say we are now going to the Polo grounds in New York and Michael O 'Hehir for the All-Ireland Final between Cavan and Kerry.

The excitement was magic and still burns brightly in Frank's memory. He remembers the crackling sound of Michael O 'Hehir coming across the air waves reporting all the way from New York. This was more exciting to Frank than the Game. Then came the clear voice of Michael O 'Hehir announcing that Bill O' Dwyer from Bohola County Mayo and the Mayor of New York would throw the ball in to start the game. It all seemed so close, occurring 3000+ miles away. Cavan went on to defeat Kerry by a score of 2-11 to 2-7.

During this period Frank's most exciting event on the farm was the harvesting of the oats and barley. Then of course there was the threshing in late October -November. This was always a big event. Frank's mother and his older sisters would cook an exceptionally large spread for the men who came to help at the threshing time. It was always a full day from dawn till dusk.

The local thresher was Joe Birrane who had a Ford Tractor and a McCormick thresher. He would arrive the day before in the late evening, get the equipment positioned and set up for the following morning. He would line up the belt and run the thresher for five to 10 minutes. He would always stay for the tea, talk, and chat with my father and older brother Paddy.

The next morning Frank's father would be up early talking to the men who had come to help: Sonny McKinley and three of his sons Tommy, John James, and often one or two of the Davis boys. Usually there would be 8-10 people. Frank's older brothers Paddy and John were now old enough to help.

Joe Birrane always started threshing before 8 am and went through lunch till dusk. Frank's mother and sisters would have a full spread of cooked bacon, turkey, duck, chicken, and goose. There would be lots of potatoes. Dessert was always rhubarb and apple pie with Bird's custard and jelly.

It was a feast the men enjoyed and, sometimes, they ate too much. John Sharp, an old bachelor, did once. Frank remembers him eating so much he had to lay down with stomach pains.

At the end of a long day Frank's father would thank the men and offer all the older ones a bottle of Guinness. The younger helpers would get a soft drink, lemonade, or orange squash. They would sit down in the glow of the tilly lamp and drink their Guinness, tell stories, and talk about the local topics. By then John Sharps pains had subsided, and he was enjoying his Guinness and the conversation.

When Frank was six years old and had begun school in the summer of 1947, he would begin to establish friendships with many new contacts outside the home and had become interested in sports. During the Summer months there were many sporting events. Those were Parish events mostly within walking distance. They would be posted in the local newspaper 'The Western People." Frank and his brothers would scour the publication June through August for the most interesting sports meetings. They would decide, based on the prize money, to go for one of the top three positions. Frank and his brother John were now extremely interested in running and were following the pursuit of the four-minute mile which was heating up in 1953.

The high prospective participants were John Landy, from Australia, Roger Bannister, from Great Britain, and Wes Santee from Kansas in the USA. Finally on a May summer's evening at Iffley road track in Oxford on May 26, 1954, Roger Bannister achieved the impossible and broke the four-minute mile with a time of 3.59.4.

This was a motivating event in the life of Frank and his older brother John. Frank was beginning to train for the summer events. He had marked out a 440 yard circle around the old derelict building they knew as The Castle, and it was around this makeshift grass running surface that he and John trained in their bare feet. They would be competing, in their dreams, with the world's greatest runners. They knew well how inadequate they were as they struggled to break 5 minutes for the mile. Gradually as the summer progressed their times improved, and they were able to compete in more distant sporting events, against stronger and better competitors.

Life was rushing by, and the village was also beginning to change.

William Spellman had died in August 1948 and Thomas in 1949. Since Thomas was Frank's godfather, he was allowed to go to the wake. Frank had just turned eight when Thomas died. Frank was sad that Thomas had died as he used to give Frank a shilling now and then for candy. The following year after Thomas died, his wife Mary gave birth to a daughter, Mary Kate. This was the last birth in the village for many years.

The vibrancy of the village was changing rapidly as the youth left for Dublin and London. By 1955, Frank was preparing to go to boarding school. His five sisters and his oldest brother Paddy had immigrated to the UK. His sisters to train as nurses and his brother to work on construction in London. Six of the   Spellman girls had also left the village. Only Patsy remained with her mother Ann, who passed the following year,1956.

That same year Frank's father's friend John [Sonny] McKinley passed away. It was an incredibly sad time for Frank's father. Frank and his two brothers, Paddy and John accompanied their father to Sonny's wake and funeral. The funeral was on a very cold winters day in February 1956. The funeral was at St Mary's [Protestant] Church of Ireland. There was a large gathering at the church. There were strangers from faraway places. All the neighbours from Sonny's village of Rathnamagh, were there, neighbours of both denominations, Protestant and Catholic. At that time in Ireland Catholics, were not allowed to attend services in a Protestant church. Some of the local Catholics remained outside the Church. Billy's father who respected the generous friendship of his old friend, turned to his boys, and said we have come this far I am attending the service of Sonny and I will say my prayer for him. Sonny was laid to rest in the church graveyard. Frank would return to St Mary's years later for a more festive occasion.

There were many sad occasions in Frank's village as the youth departed. One was in June 1957 when Patsy came by the house to say goodbye to Frank's Mother. She said she was going to Dublin. Her oldest sister, who had inherited the house and land, had sold it. Patsy had to leave Spink hill, where she used to plough land with a team of horses. It was a sad day when Patsy left the village as we would never see her again.

Frank's brother, John, left that same year to go to school in Dublin. The Village population was by then down to twelve.

Frank returned to boarding school and finished in 1960. He returned to the village for two years, leaving in the fall of 1962 for Dublin. By the time he left the village, the three Cuffe girls and one boy had also gone. The village had, by then, dwindled down to just six inhabitants.

The following year, 1963 Frank's brother John left Dublin to go to school in the USA. That same year Frank suffered a catastrophic accident and spent time in St Vincent's Hospital in Dublin where a somewhat incompetent doctor performed reconstructive surgery on his left leg. It was not a success, and he spent a further six weeks convalescing at Cappagh hospital. He recovered eventually but would never return to his former running form.

Frank struggled in Dublin trying to find a career job. He thought of joining the police force but, in the end, decided there was limited opportunity for him in Ireland.

Frank's brother John, by then in New York training for the European Games, encouraged Frank to follow him to America. Their cousin, Bernadette, had recently visited Ireland from New Jersey and suggested Frank should go to the US for a trial period to see how he would like it. She promised she would get him a job for the summer and soon, he was applying for the necessary paperwork.

In the spring of 1965 Frank made up his mind he would try it and went to the "Union of students in Ireland" at 45 Dame Street, Dublin to get a new student card, which allowed him to get the cheapest fare to Idlewild airport. He also secured an international driver's license on June 16, 1965.

Having secured the necessary paperwork Frank booked a return passage with Aer Lingus, departing July 3, nineteen sixty-five, returning September 4- that same year. The day arrived at last, and Frank's long time, friend and cousin Frank Lynn took him to Dublin Airport.

Frank boarded the plane and was pleasantly surprised that, due to overbooking, he'd been re-assigned to Buisness Class seat D-4.

He remembers the Boeing 707, rolling down the runway and slowly, or so it seemed to Frank, the plane lifted off and headed out over the Irish sea. The pilot banked left and turned west back over Dublin City. The sky was clear and visibility good. As they flew west Frank could look out the window and see below 'Santry Stadium' where he had spent the previous evening attending an international track event, staged by the great Billy Morton who had got international recognition in 1958 after setting up a race at Santry Stadium during which a new world mile record was established by Herb Elliott. The stadium was later named after Morton in recognition of his contribution to Irish sport.' On this Saturday afternoon though, as Frank headed toward America, the great Peter Snell of New Zealand, was battling with another top runner, George Kerr of Jamaica. At the time they were the world's two leading 800-meter runners.

As the plane reached cruising altitude the Pilot announced the estimated arrival time in New York, Idlewild. Frank took out his Japanese manuscript and began to read chapter seven. It was the story of an orphaned boy, who had become a great Samurai and had reached the highest level of his profession.

As he headed out, on what was intended to be a two-month visit, Frank's life was about to take a turn he would never have dreamed of and, as the Boeing 707 sped across the Atlantic he recalled the words of his mother's friend Delia, "America," she'd said. "had endless possibilities."

She was right.

Fishing
by
Killian O'Boyle

Day 1 "Can we go fishing Dad?"

Day 2 "Can we go fishing Dad?"

Day 3 "Can we go fishing Dad?"

Day 4 "Can we go fishing Dad?"

Day 5 "Will we ever go fishing Dad? Only Grandy brings me fishing!"

"Yeah, he brought you once and you caught nothing but, OK we can go fishing."

So there I am, in my 15th store, looking for a paddle board with "Shouldn't we have brought our own ones?" echoing in my ear canals.

"No, we've no paddle-boards, Lilos, rings, kayaks or anything else. Why don't you try

Decathlon?" is basically the same message in each place. So there I am looking for a 30 minute getaway from the family holiday.

"Excuse me." I say to the lifeguard outside his yellow and red hut at Portumna Marine Park. "Is there anywhere I might buy a paddle-board around here?"

"Oh" he says as he searches the middle distance for an inspired response. "Well, you could try Gary Kenny's."

"Oh yes, where's that?"

"You go back to Portumna, and then you go through the back street and onto the Main Street. Turn right there and go 2 kms till you come to the garage that isn't a garage anymore. It's got pumps but they haven't worked for years. If you get to the Emerald Star Line premises you've gone too far."

"Ah sure I might phone them so." I say.

"You'd be there as fast, driving"

"I'd be there faster if you'd stop repeating yourself." I think.

"They used to sell them at one time," he says, dashing my hopes.

"Feck", I think, as I google it. Damn, it's the same shop that he told me two days ago. Her 'big' order of 10 paddle boards was stuck in Rotterdam for the last three weeks. Still, they sell fishing tackle as well, so I'll go anyway.

An hour later, and having been into 50% of the shops in Portumna, I feel like a local. I arrive back with two lures, a nail clippers, no paddle board and a beach ball for €1.95 bought in the hardware store as a consolation prize. It's bright pink - neon - and my son spent the following 30 mins throwing it at my face as I braved the brown bog water another time. "Ouch, if you do that once more I'll ..." Homer and Bart Simpson spring to mind!

"Dad will you do a cannon ball?"

"No."

"Why not, it's so much fun."

"Cos, everyone doing cannon balls is between

the age of 7 and 12!"

"Awwwww, please, Dad."

"No. It's time to go."

The lifeguard waves us goodbye as the 10 year olds do back flips off the concrete pier behind him. One kid's head misses the pier by about two inches. The garda tarrthála says nothing. Ah sure it'll be grand!

We get home. The heat at 6pm still elicits sweat as it rolls down my nose. It's like an Italian summer.

David and I pack our fishing bag.

"Lures" - "check"

"Water" - "check"

"Life jackets" - "check"

"Knife" - "check, what do we need a knife for?"

"Kill a fish."

"Oh!"

We saunter off down the lane. The lough spreads out before us. Through the gate. Hello to the donkeys and the calves. Under the electric fence. We all got the pulse shock earlier this week. Annabelle was most put out!

The girls follow a few minutes behind giving David and I time to attach the lure to the rod's line and push the boat out into the reeds where we get stuck again. "Feck!"

Two swans and their three cygnets guide us out, although after a bit of cussing and slapping of oars they demurely glide away into the thicker reeds escaping the dastardly duo who have intentions to catch and kill a pike - the most succulent of fish - not!

I take the oars, which is fitting for my age if not necessarily my mental maturity. David acts as cox. We nearly run aground. The water is a little choppy as we pass the first island. A German family laugh gaily as they splash in the shallow waters. We go deeper. After a time, we decide it's time to start casting our lures. I demonstrate to David how to do it and successfully manage to 'catch' the incapacitated engine at the rear of the boat. Alas the previous tenants flooded the engine ensuring we couldn't get it going. Row, row, row our boat against the choppy waters. Damn! After 5 minutes the current has drifted our craft to the island's shore. Heave-ho Jeeves. That's me. More rowing, more fishing - will the torture never end? My son's romantic view of fishing as a dead cert is unravelling his innocent naivité...

Later ....

We got back. The boat is moored, the attitude is ecstatic. "Wait till we tell Mum!"

"Mum, Muuum!" he calls as we enter the house. The heat has lessened and the swallows are circling above devouring insects as they dart and dive like spitfires in battle.

"Well," says Mum, "how was it?"

"You won't believe it." David says. Annabelle's eyes immediately light up in anticipation of a great story.

"We caught a big trout. Just when Dad had

said it was time to go home, I felt a pull on the rod; it bent, and I could feel a real struggle on the end of my line. I handed it to Dad. He reeled it in and it jumped and splashed up into the boat. But we lost it!"

"What, how, why?

"When Dad cut the line, I was holding the fish and it wriggled and moved and I couldn't hold it."

Tears welled up in David's eyes he was so disappointed. "I dropped it and it swam away. Dad tried to catch it again, but got the lure caught in reeds and he had to cut the line loose"

Mum hugged him tight.

Annabelle did too.

The Break-In

by

Micheál MacSuibhne

The Cork town of Macroom is situated on the N22 road around half way between the city of Cork and Kerry town of Killarney. It sits in a valley on either side of the Sullane River, a tributary of the River Lee.

Macroom was the catchment area town for the nearby rural farming town-lands. The McCarthy's established a castle in the centre and the English had a garrison there for as long as they ruled the country.

It had two banks, two hotels, a post office and the usual smattering of shops, cafes, many pubs and a large Catholic Church.

On Tuesdays there was a livestock market located in the town square and on a Wednesday most businesses closed in the afternoon.

The town had a railway station, which linked it to Cork city until 1960.

Macroom, being a town which served the locality was also a place where people stopped to rest, eat, drink or shop as they travelled between Cork and Kerry. As a result, it was coloured by many of those from near or far who stopped on their way through it.

In 1976 local businessmen came together to established the Macroom Mountain Dew Festival, the first music festival to be held in Ireland.

It was hailed as Ireland's answer to Glastonbury and it provided the youth of Ireland with a ten day festival every summer until 1982. It attracted such names as Rory Gallagher, Marrianne Faithful, Van Morrison, Paul Young, Paul Bradey and other Irish and foreign acts at the top of their game.

With that, it also introduced the town to soft drugs and petty crime and on Good Friday, April 8th. 1977, the latter visited my family home.

I was eight years old at the time and I had two younger sisters, aged six and three. My parents were from local rural villages and settled in the town after my father secured a permanent position, teaching Book Keeping and Accounts in the town's Technical School, or Tech'.

My mother was a Primary School teacher in a rural area about eight miles outside the town in a place known best as the location of a War of Independence Ambush against the dreaded British 'Black & Tans' by the West Cork Brigade of the Irish Volunteers, led by the hero, Kevin Barry.

Hers was a two-teacher school and the oldest one in the country. It's still open today.

In the run-up to Ester Sunday, it was

religiously traditional to visit the local Church on Good Friday a number of times. The evening Vigil marked the Crucifixion of Jesus by the Jews.

During Good Friday, families would pay a visit to complete The Stations of the Cross. This involved a twelve stage journey around the inside of the church where, on the walls, there were paintings depicting the stages of the Passion of Christ, his death and resurrection. Families would recite the Rosary at each 'station'.

To us kids it seemed very dark and therefore boring. We had had to endure Mass in Latin of a Sunday and we couldn't understand why the Priest had his back to us throughout. The Catechism we were taught at school was all about kindness and honesty, yet the Clergy were aloof and austere.

We didn't have to dress in our 'Sunday best' but we did have to be well presented. The children of two teachers had to set an example and show due respect.

At lunchtime we piled into our Ford Escort for

the one mile journey to the Church on what was a bright, warn day for early April.

At the time, and for many years afterwards, 'hitching for a lift' was part of life for people who wanted to get from A to B but had no car. The road in front of our house; Gurteen Roe, was a straight stretch of about a quarter of a mile not in the town but not too far outside it either, where many 'hitched' or 'thumbed' for a lift to Killarney and further into Kerry. On any given day during the summer there could be three or four individuals or pairs out there trying to get free passage to their destination to the West and the Kingdom.

On this particular day the pair outside our gates caught my parent's attention immediately. Two young men in their twenties dressed in blue denim jeans and bright t-shirts. They had rucksacks with them and their destination was Killarney but they didn't appear to be making much of an effort. Instead, they were having their lunch. To my mother's indignation they had a catering sized tin of Corned

Beef, the sort a shopkeeper would cut slices from and they were sharing it, taking great chunks out of it as they washed it down with bottles of beer. Meat and beer on Good Friday??

To eat meat on any Friday was frowned upon but to be so blatant about it in public on Good Friday rang alarm bells in my parents' heads.

But we were committed now and we went to the Church. My parents had decided on the way there that the scene had looked 'dodgy' and on that day we retreated home from the Church after only twenty minutes of prayer. I should imagine that us kids were elated that we didn't have to stay 'for ages'!

When we arrived back that the gates of our home there was no sign of the two young men, but their rucksacks were still out on the footpath. My father unlocked and opened the from door and with that heard people moving within the house. The next thing we heard was a window being smashed in a back bedroom down the hall of the bungalow. Just inside the door was a coat and telephone stand.

The telecom's setup in Macroom in those days was that one lifted the telephone from its cradle and waited for the telephonist at the exchange, down town, to answer and after a short chat to catch up with the local gossip we could be put through to the number we wanted.

For us, the important numbers we remembered were; our own: Macroom 227, our grandparents in Kilnamartyra - 612 and my Mum's parents; Donoughmore - 15.

On this occasion there was no time for chit chat and my father asked for Macroom 27, the town's Garda Station.

As kids, we thought this was all very exciting. The thought that there might be any danger involved in having burglars in the house never crossed our minds.

When the Station Sergeant answered, my father told him that there were people in our house and one had just jumped through a window.

I'm given to understand that the reply he got was that there was "no car available".

My dad thought quickly and, as he thanked the Garda and was putting down the phone, he said to my mother, loudly enough that the Garda would hear it; "They have no car, time for the rifle."

On top of the wall mounted coat hooks Dad's .22 Rifle was kept. In the field surrounding our house he grew two acres of polythene covered strawberry plants. During the summer he would pick the ripe crop and supply them to a fruit and vegetable wholesaler in Cork. It paid for our holidays in Kerry every summer, as well as a few other treats. The rifle was necessary to shoot a few crows and hang their corpses from stakes in the field so as to warn off other crows attracted by the strawberries.

It also turned out that it put the fear of God into local kids who might like to help themselves to our valuable fruit.

The second 'robber' had left the house via the

back door, which had been forced in earlier so they could gain access. The trouble they now found themselves in was that they were at the back of the house and the only way out of the property was through our front gate. My mother was there and she was very angry.

They decided it would be better to run to the bottom of our field and scale the hedge row. They ran like lunatics, and one of them had something in his hand.

They hadn't noticed that the hedge they were headed for was a Blackthorn. Its long spiked needles were not the easiest to get through and, while one man got over it quite readily, the other ended up being delayed as he was badly scratched and cut.

My mother lead us children out onto the footpath and we saw one, about a hundred yards away, emerge out onto the path from the neighbouring farmer's field. He ran to the west but, instead of staying on the main road, he took the fork to the right, towards the outskirts area called Codrum.

A moment later, the second burglar, who was limping, arrived out onto the footpath. With that, an unmarked car owned by a Garda sped past us at the gate. It was driven at great speed towards the escaping thieves. I will never forget seeing Garda Connor Byrne jump from the moving vehicle onto the limping man trying to make his escape. It was like something out one of the American cops and robbers we would have seen on television!

The Garda driving the car carried on and veered right and headed towards Codrum.

A short while later and actual Garda Squad Car arrived and first collected the further detainee and returned for the injured party. That car was being driven by the Station Sergeant and he returned to the entrance to our home to collect the rucksacks which had been left behind. He also wanted to 'have a word' with my dad.

"I was worried, "he said, when Dad went over to meet him. "I thought you said you were going to use a rifle."

"Oh did you?" my father answered, smiling. "I thought *you* said you didn't have any cars!"

The rifle, of course, had never left its resting place!

A fortnight later, and the two thieves were before the District Court in Macroom where they were left off with a Caution.

My father was furious. The back door frame had been damaged, a large bedroom window had been smashed, and a bottle of Brandy had been taken, along with a £20 note my mother had hidden 'for a rainy day'. No mention of any compensation was made in Court.

The following day the parents of one of the burglars arrived to our door. They were repentant, on behalf of their son, and paid for the damage to the window and door and handed my father a bottle of Brandy and a £20 note.

A few days later a retired Garda from Codrum knocked on our door. He explained that he had been out cutting the grass in his front garden that afternoon and found a full bottle of Brandy beneath the hedge. A non-drinker, he asked neighbours; and it didn't take him long to find out who owned it.

The following day my dad visited the home of the repentant parents of the young man in Cork City and returned to them the bottle of Brandy they had delivered on behalf of their son.

No more was said of it!

Un été en Suisse

by

Patricia Storey

I suppose everyone has memories of their first job. I certainly do, and not just because it was the first one. I was still at school when it all came up, well college really - a Language and Secretarial school I'd gone to straight after my Leaving Certificate. I was seventeen.

It was all rather odd really; in the middle of a dual French and Secretarial skills course, and part of it, I had to spend three months living in a French speaking household in a French speaking country. This was something I was not happy about; I was very much a 'home bird' at that stage of my life when tasting, and not very much enjoying, the greater freedoms that come with adulthood. Everyone is apprehensive about where they are going when they are at that age, and I was particularly sensitive to the leap that would soon take me from my home, my parents and my sisters.

Miss Brophy, the principal of the college, called me in one day to say she had not received my answer to the application for a French speaking three-month summer job that I had been given the previous week. It would be one I'd have to complete so she could find me a place in France or Switzerland where I could get the necessary exposure to the French language, and where I could start putting into practice some of the conversational skills I had been gathering during the rest of my first three terms.

'And,' she added, 'You knew that working abroad in a French speaking country is an essential part of the course, and that without it you won't be able to proceed into Second Year.'

I was very distressed, a bundle of nerves, I

did not want to go abroad on my own for a day, let alone three months. I vacillated, what was I to do? I knew that if I told my dad he'd try to talk me into doing as Miss Brophy had asked. Mum would perhaps have been more understanding of my nervousness, especially of being thrust amongst people neither she or I knew, let alone ones who only spoke French, at which I was still a novice.

I tossed and turned at night, unable to sleep as I tried to force myself to agree to do what I had been asked. And then, a few days later, as I was passing through the college hall, I unexpectedly found myself face to face with Miss Brophy, and my heart all but stopped. 'Ah, Patricia,' she said, 'have you filled in that application form yet ... today is the last day?'

'Erm ... no ... not yet, Miss.'

'You are leaving it a bit late Patricia. If you don't return the application form by the end of the week you will be leaving us without a qualification at the end of the term. It is not possible to continue into second year unless you have completed three months in a French speaking home.

'Yes Miss Brophy,' I replied, almost in tears.

***

'What was I to do?' I asked my best friend, Alison, who'd been in my class at secondary school and had first introduced the idea of a secretarial and foreign language school to me. She had already got herself fixed up with an 'overseas' three-month French speaking summer job.

'Dad'll kill me if I mess this up' I said.

Another restless night … and I still hadn't given the application form to my father to fill in. And then, Sod's Law, as I entered the college the next morning, I bumped into Miss Brophy again.

'Well, Patricia?' she asked. 'Have you that form for me, the latest day to apply for one of the positions listed is today. If I don't get your response by this evening, you will not be able to go into second year with your friends, and in order to win your certificate you'll have to repeat the academic year you are just finishing.'

I couldn't think of what to say … and then, clutching at the proverbial straws, and just as I was about to burst into tears, I blurted out, 'Alison's mum is getting me a job.'

It was a ridiculous answer to give her; I'd never even met Alison's mother.

Miss Brophy, smiling, seemed to accept the outrageous lie I had just told her and, fearful of the consequences of my behaviour, I went to find Alison to tell her what had happened.

To my surprise she laughed, and then, as though to shrug the whole incident off, she said. 'Don't worry, Mum'll sort something out; she has loads of friends who speak French.'

And she did, she got me fixed up with people in Switzerland she knew who, she said, would be writing to me to confirm dates and so on.

It all seemed so unreal; one minute I was going to be ejected from the course at the end of term, the next I was going to live with a family in Switzerland, where I'd be helping a grandmother look after her four month old grandson so that her daughter (the child's mother) could accompany her husband (a university professor) on a long lecture tour in South Africa.

When I got home, I casually told my mother and father that I had obtained a job in Switzerland through Alison's mother, and that I'd be starting as soon as the term ended.

My father looked at me doubtfully, 'But who are these people who have offered you a job, Patricia.' he asked, 'We can't just let you go swanning out into the blue; we need to know something about them and about the terms of employment you have been offered.'

I couldn't answer, because I didn't know myself, and the tears started again.

Mum, ever the calmer of emotions, put her arm round me and wisely suggested that we wait until we'd seen what the woman in Switzerland put in her letter. Dad nodded and retired to the sitting room, a glass of whiskey in his hand to calm him down. He'd agreed with Mum's suggestion but he definitely wasn't happy.

And things stayed like that until one day, towards the end of the week, when I got in from college, Mum all but overwhelmed with curiosity, gave me an envelope that had arrived in that morning's post, addressed to me. On the back flap of it, what seemed to be a very fancy coat of arms was embossed. And inside, in a spidery hand, the terms of my prospective three-month job were spelled out. As I remember they mostly concerned me telling the writer what I could and could not eat, what formal clothing I had, and how much money I was to be paid. It didn't ask if I had any experience with babies or if I could cook. More important, it seemed, was whether or not I had at least three changes of evening dress. This was weird, but the crest on the envelope re-assured us a little. It seemed I was being asked to join a very distinguished household for the summer.

And so it turned out. Looking after the baby was fun and not too difficult, as my employer spent most of her time with the little one and I anyway. We travelled around visiting grand relatives and attending reunions of her husband's family, most of whom dwelt in a very different world to mine.

But it really was fun. I'll never forget going shopping and being embarrassed at my employer's antics as she scooted round on a supermarket trolley, one foot hopping, and the other resting on the rear axle shield. She was always bumping into shelves and displays, and on one day that I will never forget, she crashed into a big pyramid of cans containing pulped tomatoes, scattering them all along the aisle. She seemed to like acting like a naughty school-child and, surprisingly, the people in the supermarket didn't appear to mind. I suppose they got a lot of kudos by having such a distinguished person as one of their customers.

Going there to buy food was a regular necessity, obviously, but to buy pot noodles only, as she seemed to do, I thought was absolutely 'nuts' as well as being boring. I don't think I've eaten one since. Her husband, working in an underground garage at home, and restoring ex-World War Two American army jeeps, was just as odd ... and just as kind ... a lovely man. Getting these war-worn vehicles, and he had several, back into working order to add to his collection had become his mission in life, a distraction from the disruption that had come to it at the end of the war.

It was all he had left to do by then ... mend vehicles as broken as himself. For, until a few years earlier, he'd been the King of one of Europe's great nations, one of several that were taken over by communists at the end of the Second World War; deposing him and making him a 'persona non grata' in his own land.

The 'mad' woman who'd crashed into the tower of tomatoes in the supermarket and lived on pot noodles had been his Queen, and the baby grandson I'd been brought in to help look after, was the Crown Prince. I could hardly take it all in.

When I returned home for my second year at Miss Brophy's at the end of the summer, and met my friends from the previous year back for the new term, I soon established that most of them had 'au paired'.

I knew they wouldn't believe me if I told them of my adventure, so I kept my extraordinary story to myself.

Even to this day I doubt any of them, except Alison, would have accepted my story was true had I told it to them. But it is; I've still got the letter … I've still got the memories … and I've still got a photograph showing a middle-aged couple, both easily identifiable, sitting on an ornate garden bench taking tea. The woman is holding a baby at whom the man is smiling. Sitting between them is a slim, shy looking teenage girl in a blue dress. And "Yes", even after all these years, it is easy to see … it's me.!

Lent 1961

by

Pat Mullan

In the kitchen, my mother was on her hands and knees, the 'bag apron' on, scrubbing the cracked concrete kitchen floor. She came up to her knees as I handed her the letter that came in the post. The 'bag apron', with Sow and Weaner Pig Meal on the front, was saturated with sudsy water around her knees while the baby slept on in the cot in the corner. I headed upstairs to the boys' bedroom with another few sticky *Liquorice All-sorts* sweets that I'd got from George the postman, to add to my collection.

It was the fifth week into Lent, just two more weeks until it was over. I was looking forward to gorging on my collection on Easter Sunday - the Jelly Babies and *Liquorice Allsorts* from George the Post, the half packet of Spangles that Aunt Maggie had brought between me and my sister, Margaret. And, best of all, the two chocolate marshmallows that my mother had bought me. All safety stored in the blue and white National Dried Milk tin, with the Ministry for Food written on it, buried under all the old coats and bedclothes in the old pram behind the bed headboard in our bedroom.

I pulled out the tin. No jelly-babies, one marshmallow and nothing left of the Spangles but the wrapping. The tears welled. I checked that I'd got the right tin; the one with P M scratched on the tin's lid with a nail. No mistaking that. A good hiding place that had served me well for all sorts of things, had been discovered and raided. And I knew who the culprit was. She'd pay for this, by Jeekers!

"What's wrong, son?" my mother asked, standing up from her work as I trudged into the kitchen, head down.

The tears welled again. Embarrassed, "Nothing," I said.

"That's not like you, son. What's wrong? Come here," she repeated as she took me in her arms.

The unstoppable sobs came then. "She took all my sweets," I managed to say between uncontainable outbursts. "It's not fair. And she broke Lent."

My mother patted my back and ran her fingers soothingly through my hair. "Don't worry, we'll soon sort Margaret out, won't we?"

I brightened. "What will we do?" I asked.

"Just you wait and see." she replied. "Come on. It's time to feed the pigs."

In the boiling house, I poured the water from the hose into the buckets while my mother stirred and beat the concoction into a watery slurpy mess using the mixing iron. Then she carried the two big enamel buckets to the pig house. You could hear the squeals of excitement from the pig-house as the pigs, by then nearly 4 months old, heard the rattle of the buckets. I opened the door for her and made sure none of the pigs escaped. As soon as the feed was poured into the long trough the squealing abated as the pigs concentrated on the work in hand; all lined up at right angles to the trough as they slurped the meal into their hungry mouths. I ran along the line straightening out the pigs' tails one after the other, but they immediately and automatically recoiled back to their original curled up position.

We then climbed the stone barn steps and collected the eggs and brought them into the pantry.

"Come here, son," my mother said. "See what I found." She took the lid off the big 40-gallon wooden barrel churn that we kept the flour in. She reached deep into the flour and came up with a National Dried Milk tin and showed me the initials scratched on the lid. M.M. She winked at me and touched the side of her nose three time. Then she put the tin back where she had found it and covered it back over with flour.

I never went near the flour barrel again until that Holy Saturday night, when I sneaked out to the barrel-churn, recovered what I had lost, and took a bit more as compensation.

It was the best Easter I ever had.

The Jumble Sale

by

Susie Knight

As a child I lived with my Mother, Grandmother, Grandfather and two Uncles in a small house on the outskirts of East London.

I was in the Brownies, which I loved. I was the leader or Sixer of 'The Gnomes'. There were other Sixes or groups including Pixies, Fairies and Imps. Brownies were required to learn and recite a Brownie Promise and a Law. The Promise was 'I Promise to do my best, to do my duty to God and the Queen, to help other people, especially those at home. The Law was 'Be Prepared'!

Each Six had a special song. The Gnome's song was 'Here you see the laughing Gnomes, helping

Mothers in their homes'! I expect that this song has changed now, as it rather implies that a girl's life is 'In the home'! Not much equality promoted in this structure at that time!

I did love going to Brownies on Tuesday evenings. I guess I was about seven on this particular Tuesday evening. We all gathered in a circle and said The Promise and the Law and sang our songs and saluted. Then Brown Owl announced that we would be having a jumble sale in a few weeks' time, to raise funds. She said that we would all have to collect as much jumble as possible and bring it to the hall on the Saturday of the sale. She also announced that there would be a prize for the Brownie who collected the most jumble!

Well, the challenge was on! I was determined to win that prize and I went home thinking about how I was going to do it. I mused, that knocking on doors unannounced and asking for Jumble was not very efficient. People needed time to search for it, as it was usually hidden away! So, it seemed to me that you needed a 'System'. You needed to be organised and make appointments with people, telling them about the sale and then booking dates and times to go back to collect the goods.

The next day I gathered all my friends together for a meeting. I told them about the challenge and asked them if they wanted to help.

. They did, so I had a team of six including me! I told them that they would need their dolls' prams for collecting jumble. We decided to work in pairs. I allocated each pair a list of roads. I explained that they would have to first visit each house and give the person a note saying what the Jumble Collection was for. Then they would agree a date and a time to return to that house to collect the haul!

We wrote out sheets with all the roads on, so we could record when to do our collections.

We also wrote out hundreds of flyers to take

to the houses we hoped to visit. I found some carbon paper, which made this easier. But it was still hard work.

I asked my grandmother if we could store the jumble in the conservatory of her house and she agreed! She had no idea what this would entail.

On the day we decided to start, we were all very excited. We met by my back gate with our dolls' prams, clipboards and flyers! We were off. We met back at the gate at lunchtime and everyone said that it had gone really well and that they had loads of bookings for us to return.

I told them that they must tell me if they could not make any of the appointments, so we could get someone else to go. I told them it was really important to turn up on time! How I knew this, I am not sure.

After a few days the collections began. There were dolls' prams loaded up with stuff careering down the roads all over the village. They then turned up at my back gate, where we stored all the 'stuff'. My grandmother was horrified as the pile started to get bigger and bigger. She began to worry that some of the stuff might be dirty or flea ridden! But still it kept coming.

The system was working very well! People had tidied their cupboards and got bags of stuff ready for collection. After four days the conservatory was half full and my uncles had to help to pack it in up to the ceiling. There were shoes and bags, and old books, a couple of typewriters, and lots of clothes!

My own collection area was on the other side of the main arterial road in and out of London, known as the A13. I carefully crossed the road during the afternoon and went to do my collections. I got a lot of stuff, including a huge wicker clothes basket. It was very difficult to balance this on my dolls' pram with all the other stuff as well.

It was about five o'clock and I needed to get

home. I got to the traffic lights and realised that it was rush hour and the traffic in and out of London was very busy. The lights turned green and I hurried to cross, holding the clothes basket on the top of the pram. Just as I got to the middle of the road, the pram tipped over and everything fell out! The lights had changed, but no one could go. Cars were hooting and I started to panic. My pram was upside down in the middle of the road with its wheels spinning and there were clothes everywhere

At that moment, a Policeman arrived, and he helped to sort it all out and got me safely across the road. He asked me where I was going with all the stuff. I said I was collecting jumble to sell to make money for our funds.

At this moment, by pure chance, my uncle pulled into the side of the road. He got out and asked what was going on? The Policeman explained and my uncle looked horrified! He packed all the jumble, the pram and me into his car and took me home.

My grandmother was not impressed with what had happened or with more 'Old Toot' as she called it! It was all getting a bit out of hand. But there were only two more days to go and the jumble still kept coming.

On the Saturday morning, my uncle packed his car to the roof eight times! My Brown Owl was delighted with the amount of stuff I had collected. The sale was a great success.

At the end of the afternoon, Brown Owl announced the winner of the prize for collecting the most jumble. I so hoped it would be me – and it was! I went up to get my prize and she told the assembled crowd about my plan for the whole exercise and told the story about me holding up all the traffic on the main road. Everyone laughed and clapped, and I went very red. But I also had a glow in my tummy, and that was the best reward.

I don't remember what the prize was or how I thanked and rewarded my team. However, I did do something, because I instinctively knew that if you want people to do something for you, you have to make them feel appreciated. I think, overall, that I was less of a 'Laughing Gnome' and more a Wily Old Fox!

An Unexpected Discovery

by

Verell Booth

Dear Peggie,

I hope your arthritis isn't giving you too much trouble. Mine is 'killing' me but I got a good laugh yesterday that, for the moment, put all thoughts of old age and illness out of my mind. You'll never believe this but when I turned on the radio to listen to the news the previous programme was still running and a man was reading from Bleak House, my favourite Dickens story. Hearing the words as he read them, prompted me to reach for a copy of Bleak House I knew was in The Golden Treasury Dickens collection I got for my tenth birthday but seldom open these days. I intended to skip through a few pages to refresh my recollection what I have always considered to be Dickens's most enthralling story.

To my surprise, when I dusted off the book and opened it, a letter fell out. It must have been put there by me ninety years ago by the date on it, and I got my grandson to photograph it and forward it to you as I can never remember how to do it.

When you read what I put in that letter all those years ago, you'll laugh. But you'll also see why I never sent it. Now, with all that time between when I wrote it and today, I suppose it doesn't matter.

Ring me when you've read it, and we can have a good laugh over the incident which, incidentally, is still quite clear in my mind. Cousin Verell was a conceited bitch let's face it, and she was one right to the end in my judgement ... too pompous by far for my humble branch of the family; a really unpleasant person.

As to the remark I made about Billy, my guess was right, wasn't it? He did fancy you ... which probably explains why he's been married to you for the last eighty years!

Please give him my best wishes.

Hope to see you soon,

Love,

Verell.

See attachment:

September 1934

Dear Peggie,

I hope you are well. Sorry I haven't written to you sooner, but as you will see, I didn't have much time to sit down and write letters!

You remember I told you these cousins on Dad's side were coming to stay, and how excited we were about it? Well, we got a big disappointment. There's the mother and two children alright, but the children are OLD, he's about thirty and she's twenty four, and all done up with lipstick and green stuff round her eyes, she looks weird!

They live in Cambridge, she - that's the daughter - has the same name as me, Verell, and, would you believe it, she brought her dog with her. He's a black Scottie, called "Angie Man", at least that's what she calls him, in a silly squeaky voice, I think it's really Angus, and she has him sitting behind her on her chair at mealtimes. She was even giving out because she wasn't allowed to bring him into the cinema with her! Stupid eejit, who'd want to bring a dog to the Pictures! Our poor Binkie doesn't get a look in and he's a much nicer dog and I'm sure his feelings are hurt, though he has been very good putting up with it all.

Anyway, she was going on about her horse-riding, in some posh riding place, in Cambridge, indoor, with a 'tan', that's a sort of floor made with peat, I think, and said she couldn't wait to ride in Ireland. So my Dad made enquiries and found a riding stable in the Rocky Valley. He made an appointment for us to go there the day before yesterday. Dad let Morton, the brother, drive his car, and my bro, Peter, his pal Mickey and the two Verells, me and her, went along to the stable. Morton went for a drive to see the countryside.

Verell was all togged up with riding gear, boots and breeches etc. I had a pair of jodhpurs from that shop Millets, they were only cheap, but they do all right. Peter just had his shorts. When we got there, it didn't look very posh, just stables and a farm yard, and a couple of big fields behind it. The owner of the place brought out the horses and gave the biggest one to Verell, not me, the cousin. We went out into the field, Mickey wasn't riding, he just came along. We were all looking at Verell, expecting her to be great at riding, after all her talk; she has been looking down her nose at us because we are 'only kids' she says.

To start with, her horse wouldn't do more than walk, while we trotted around the field in great style, showing off. Then because she was complaining that she couldn't get going, Mickey pulled up a stem of rag weed, and whacked her horse on its bottom. Well, it certainly got going then, and galloped madly along while she clung onto the reins, holding them up in the air instead of keeping them low. We yelled at her to keep her hands down, but she didn't listen, silly ass! She can't have learned very much at the marvellous riding school. Of course, we were in stitches, even when she fell off into the ditch. It's a wonder we didn't fall off too, we were laughing so much. She wasn't hurt, but of course she blamed the horse. Then, yesterday, we were to have gone riding again, but she said she wasn't going to go, she was too sore. We said you should always get up on a horse again if you fall, but she said it wasn't because she fell, she was just too sore. I think it serves her jolly well right for boasting like that. She's a pain. I felt like saying "Pride comes before a fall" but thought I'd better not, because she's a guest. The brother is nice though, even though he's old. I'll be glad when they go home and we won't have to be on our best behaviour. Mum says we were mean to laugh at Verell, and very rude, but I bet she would have thought it was funny too.

That's all the news - oh, I nearly forgot to tell you; Billy next door was asking about you, I think he likes you!!

Looking forward to seeing you soon,

Love,

Verell.

xxx

A Surprise from the Skies

By

Alan Grainger

O ne afternoon, back in August 1941, I think it must have been, Nobby Clarke, Jack Dinsdale … and I, got a surprise we will never forget; I doubt it'll ever be forgotten by anyone else living in the town at the time either.

To set the scene, I'll have to go back eighty years, to a sunny afternoon in May or June of that year, and a picnic my mother and sister Susan and I were having on the lawn in the back garden of our Surrey home.

I was about thirteen years old at the time, and fully alert to the fact I was living in a war-zone.

Hardly a day passed when the air-raid siren on the roof of our local police station didn't rev up to blast out the high-pitched undulating whine everybody dreaded ... for it signalled another enemy air attack was imminent.

The air raid warning could go off at any time - day or night - but, on that particular day, it had been silent until we were sitting on the lawn, eating mock egg sandwiches my mother had made by liberally salting and peppering slices of bread and margarine, and folding them into sandwiches which, in some miraculous way, tasted of egg ... or so she told us!

We looked up from our picnic instinctively the minute the siren sounded, fear already gnawing at our thoughts.

And there they were - almost overhead - planes - two of them - one of them a German Heinkel 111 bomber.

It seemed to be heading south to the coast. And the other, an RAF Spitfire that was right on his tail ... and firing at him.

In seconds they'd gone. And then we heard more bombers ... and they sounded as if they were coming our way too, as they hot-footed it in the direction of the coast fifty miles south of us, pursued by our fighters.

My mother sensed the danger first and leapt from the rug upon which we'd been sitting. Then, grabbing my hand, and Susan's, she yanked us to our feet and ran us the few yards to the entrance of our air-raid shelter; an amazing eight-foot, by eight-foot, by eighteen-foot concrete box that had been cast in a hole dug over the weekends of 1938 and '39 by Dad and me and the man next door.

We'd barely squeezed in through the manhole entrance when the first of the bombs landed. It had probably been dropped by one of the bombers to lighten its load and give it more manoeuvrability, higher speed, and a better chance of escaping the Spitfires and Hurricanes that were after it with their guns blazing. The noise was both deafening and terrifying.

The lights in the shelter must have failed when the first bomb landed, and we had to grope our way deeper into our man-made haven. The noise of each explosion was ear shattering, and the upheaval that followed it, rocked us so much we couldn't stay on our feet. Instead, we were sent sprawling to the floor or tipped onto one of the sleeping shelves built into the shelter's wall.

And still the bangs and shuddering continued. More and more bombs exploding as the enemy departed.

We thought the house had been demolished; its parts thrown into the air before falling upon us in a cascade of broken bricks, and burying us … alive … under a mound of rubble that had once been our home.

And then it stopped and everything went quiet … deathly quiet.

Mother was the first on her feet, and she felt around for the battery powered emergency light, while Susan and I were picking ourselves up from the floor. Too frightened to speak or cry, we sat on the edge of our beds, waiting to see if we could hear more bombers coming our way.

We couldn't, thank Goodness, so we slowly opened the hatch and climbed out of the shelter, by then covered in a mass of debris, expecting to see our home flattened.

It wasn't, in fact it looked untouched. The broken bricks, tiles and bits of furniture scattered all over our garden must have been thrown right over our house and the one next door, by a series of massive explosions that had taken place on the other side of the road!

We walked up the garden and went out to the front of the house through the side gate.

The opposite side of the road was a great big heap of smoking rubble. Fourteen houses reduced to a pile of broken masonry, chimney pots, shattered glass and splintered woodwork. Perched on top of the remnants of the Davis's bungalow, directly opposite my bedroom window, and as though it had been placed there, was Mrs Davis's treadle driven Singer sewing machine.

Miraculously, there was only one fatality; a neighbour's dog. It had been trapped in the collapsed remains of its home and died when it breathed in gas escaping from a broken main.

We were still checking for damage to the roof and front of our house when Dad suddenly appeared, having had to weave his way through a conglomeration of rescue service vehicles and personnel to get home. He didn't waste time, he told us to pack our bags, that the next day he was going to send us up to my grandmother's, out of danger, in Leyburn, a little market town nearly two hundred miles away in the middle of Wensleydale in Yorkshire (later made famous as the location for a TV series built round the life of a country vet called Dr Herriot).

Inserted into a community that did not know me, I found it hard to make friends at first. In fact, I must have been a bit of a curiosity to the Leyburn boys. But sharing bits of shrapnel I'd picked up in my own garden down in Surrey, telling of dog fights overhead between our Spitfires and Hurricanes and the German 109 and 110 Messerschmitt's, as well as describing the horror of seeing a plane spiralling to the ground with its pilot drifting down behind it suspended by his parachute, soon saw me admitted to the most prestigious gang. It was run jointly by Nobby Clarke, whose father was the local Lloyd's Bank manager, and Jack Dinsdale, son of Leyburn's slaughterman.

Getting into Nobby and Jack's gang was not easy but, as mentioned, keen to hear a first-hand account of what it was like to be bombed out, to experience the tingling excitement of watching planes in an ariel scrap, with some shot down and a some with their pilots bailing out, I soon found myself included on their expeditions.

These could be to watch Jack's dad, through a crack in the wooden wall of his small slaughterhouse, as he despatched animals with a bolt gun or pole axe and, in the case of sheep, hung them up to bleed out after he'd cut their throats.

I'll never forget seeing one of his assistants removing a sheep's intestine. He ran it between his fingers to squeeze out the digested food before coiling it round his arm as you might coil a rope. Later that day I learned, to my disgust, it would be used to make sausage skins.

I got my nickname around then - 'Gringo'; a derivation of my surname that Nobby conjured up one day when we were rabbiting.

The most extraordinary changes of the many that came into my life as a result of going to live in Leyburn, was that when I got there I only went to school in the afternoons.

Arriving at my grandmother's after driving through London, still blazing from the previous night's bombing, and a long train journey, I found an approach to the Headmaster of Yorebridge Grammar

School, twelve miles farther up the dale, had already been made. He'd explained to my grandmother that the school buildings were being used by two, two hundred pupil, grammar schools; his own ... and one from West Hartlepool, a coastal town bordering a huge manufacturing area that included Newcastle, Sunderland, Middlesbrough and Stockton ... all committed to the manufacture of war weapons and the building of ships. And all obvious targets for the Luftwaffe.

The pupils and teachers from Hartlepool were billeted in households in the nearby villages of Aysgarth, Hawes and Askrigg. And they used the school in the mornings from eight until one. After that, the pupils and staff of *our* school took the classrooms over until 6 pm ... which was well after dark in the wintertime.

When I was enrolled into Yorebridge Grammar, I found my life much changed; I had every morning free for a start. But the joy of gaining that was more than balanced by the misery of taking the twelve thirty pm train from Leyburn, in order to be in my classroom at one fifteen. At the end of the school day, I'd return to Leyburn by the six thirty bus which would get me back to my grandmother's at around a quarter past seven - depending on the weather - for in the winter we could get six feet of snow.

These were very strange times for me but, rather surprisingly, I soon got used to them.

Those days in Leyburn were amongst the most memorable of my life. Around two hundred miles from London, as I have said, the war seemed a world away. And it wasn't just a matter of a change of location for me, there were lots of other differences that cropped up, including the change in my name that I had to get used to; some of them were pleasurable … some were not.

I got my first part time job for instance, as a drover at the local cattle market, where my uncle was the auctioneer. Very apprehensive when I began there, and quite scared of the larger animals, I was soon 'Hey upping' with the rest of them as I tapped or poked the backside of the slowest moving cattle or sheep with my hazel stick. This would be when they were being driven to the slaughterhouse, the holding pens in the station yard, or, if they were lucky, a local farmer's field.

I made a couple of shillings some days - two weeks pocket money in one go. Fabulous. And I made new friends in that cattle market too, local boys who were using their wages to finance the purchase of foreign stamps, air gun pellets, banana split, treacle toffee, black striped teeth wrecking humbugs, and bottles of orange coloured Tizer.

We used to spend a lot of time on the river banks too, fishing for trout with worms and occasionally catching one; shooting at rabbits with our air rifles and almost invariably missing them … or snaring them … which was more successful. We'd sell them to the local butcher after skinning them and selling the pelts to a woman who made gloves. And, of course, we played war games, a lot of 'Bang bang you're dead' sort of stuff. All kids did and, as you might expect, nobody wanted to be the enemy.

It was on one morning, when we were skirmishin up on the moor, over towards the army firing range at Bellerby, an area we often visited when we were looking for empty shell cases and bits of grenades, that we got the shock of our lives.

We'd met early, around half past eight. It was bright and sunny, and there was warmth in the air when we set off on that amazing day.

Our intention had been to go straight to the boundary stone wall of the firing range, and climb through a gap we'd made in it, before pressing on to the old ruin known as Rock Castle, which never seemed to me to be much more than an old stone barn surrounded by oak trees.

It was a favourite place for us, and we often used it as our headquarters which, of course, we had to defend against enemy attacks when we were playing war games.

Sometimes it might be the HQ of a contingent of German soldiers, and we'd creep up on it, our weapons in our hands, and shoot the lot.

Jack had an old air gun he'd borrowed from his brother; I had a 'nearly new' one I'd bought with my cattle droving and birthday money, and Nobby had a catapult with elastic so strong it could fire a pebble farther than our air guns could shoot a pellet.

Down on our knees we'd gradually crawl nearer and nearer, and then, at the last minute, we'd leap up and charge into the building screaming like Dervishes, running from room to room, and terrifying any sheep that had nipped in for a nap. It was great fun.

On other days we'd slip round the back and surprise the enemy by entering the castle by a creaky old half door ... and killing all before us. Going in by the rear entrance meant we'd have to go through the oak trees, from the branch of one of which, we'd fashioned a swing by hanging an old car tyre on a rope.

It was on one of the days on which we'd chosen to attack through those big old oaks that we saw him. He was suspended from a high up branch of one of the trees by the cords of his parachute … an airman in his flying overalls, blood all over his face and dangling, limply … though from his groans we could tell he was alive.

Jack saw him first … and pointed. I can remember the shock I got when I looked up and saw what he'd just spotted. Nobby blurted out what we were all thinking. 'He's a Gerry; I bet he's a Gerry. He must have got shot down last night.'

'What'll we do? I asked. 'He looks all but dead to me; he must have been caught by the guns at Catterick and bailed out before his plane went down … I wonder where it is?'

As I spoke the man's eyes opened and he began to mumble quietly.

'What's he saying?' asked Jack.

'Don't know.' Nobby answered, 'but we'd better get someone.'

Jack turned to me then, 'What's he saying Gringo? Come on … ask him who he is … you 'do'

German; me and Nobby don't.'

'Me? ... German? ... Crikey, I'm not sure I can; I only got twenty percent in last week's test.'

'Go on ... try him, say some German ... let's see what he does.'

I shouted up to the man who'd closed his eyes again by then. 'Hey Mister ... are you German?' Are you Deutscher? Bist du Deutscher?'

He flicked a hand up, though his eyes were still closed, 'Ja ja ... ich bin Deutscher.'

'Er ... er ... we'd better get help then.' said Jack, clearly surprised to find that I actually *could* speak a few words of the airman's language.

The German opened his eyes and pointed to the harness cords that were wrapped round the branch way up above him ... and signalled a scissor cut with his fingers.

'Come on then,' said Nobby, 'we'd better get down to the farm and tell them what's happened.'

'He might escape while we're gone.'

'Don't be daft,' said Jack. 'how? ... No ...

two of us can stay here and make sure he doesn't get away … and one can run down to the farm and get help. O.K.? Me and Gringo'll stay here and guard him; he can see we have guns. You get down to the farm as quick as you can Nobby, and get some help.'

'Why me?' Nobby asked. 'Why can't I guard him?'

'What … with a catapult … don't be daft.'

And that's what we did. Jack and I stayed and made sure the German airman didn't wriggle free and escape, and Nobby, somewhat reluctantly, ran for help. He was back in twenty minutes.

The Gerry had slipped back into unconsciousness again by then, and was slowly twisting around as he dangled.

Sergeant Lawson, all self-important and holding his truncheon up as if he were about to strike the first person he met, puffed into sight some thirty minutes later.

His eyes nearly popped out of his head when

he saw Fritz (for that's what Jack and I had started calling the poor sod dangling above us) and he stood, sweating profusely, trying to work out what to do. 'We need a ladder.' He said ... eventually. 'Go and find a ladder boys; there must be one here somewhere.'

'There's no ladder Sergeant; we've looked.'

'Right ... no effin' ladder ... OK ... here's what we'll do.' he said, pulling a penknife from his pocket and, with a horny nicotine-stained thumbnail, levered out the largest blade. 'We'll pull over a few of those half rotten bales of straw by the wall, cut 'em open and spread 'em out below him. Then, one of you can climb up the tree and cut him free. And for God's sake put those air rifles down, you'll injure somebody.'

Jack looked at him dubiously ... so did I ... but Fritz, semi-conscious again, hung silently ... watching us.

Well ... we did get him down ... and he wasn't too badly injured either; just a few deepish cuts on his face and forehead; wounds he'd probably sustained when the plane was hit. And a broken leg he must have got when the parachute cords were cut and he fell onto the mouldy old straw bales we'd put down to catch him.

I'll never forget his face though; it was screwed up in pain as he lay motionless on the straw. It could have been an attempt at a heroic smile of course … but it was probably a leer. I'd have found out if the Civil Defence team hadn't come charging up from the farm on a tractor … a trailer bouncing along behind them with Nobby trying to hang onto it.

'Come on lads.' said the Sergeant, as the First-aiders took over, 'Best leave 'em to it.'

Recognising our moment of glory was over, we reluctantly picked up our air guns and set off back to our homes.

Down below, at the bottom of the sloping twenty acre field, the twelve thirty for Askrigg was slowly pulling out of the station.

'Great.' Said Jack. 'There'll be no school for

us today then. Let's go and find some rabbits.'

Nobby nodded … 'Yeah … I'm on …'

'Me too.' I said… giving a farewell wave to the train and shouting 'Auf Wiedersehen' at the top of my voice.

The head of the council wrote us a letter a few days later, and several people said we ought to get a medal. But that'd be stupid; we didn't do anything except watch a poor German airman's face as it gradually dawned on him it'd be ages before he'd see his family again.

Amazingly, a few years later, long after the war was over and right out of the blue, he turned up again, Fritz. Which is when we discovered his real name was Heinrich … Heinrich Scheffler.

He just walked into Jack's butcher's shop and announced himself; said he was in the area on holiday and staying at The Bull in Aysgarth. He had his wife and kids with him. Jack rang me to see if there was any chance I could get up from London so we could all meet up. But I had commitments and couldn't make it. Nor could Nobby; he'd emigrated to Australia as soon as the war in the Far East was over. It was disappointing, naturally; but Jack and I, not to be put off, began to plan a meeting for the following year.

Somehow *it* never happened either and, within a year or two, the connection between us was down to Christmas cards only. Even that didn't last. I haven't heard from either of them for years.

I often wonder if Rock Castle is still there, and if kids still play war games in it like we used to. I don't suppose they do. No, these days they'll more likely be found glued to a war game on their computer. They'd get a hell of a shock if a parachutist suddenly dropped in though, wouldn't they?!

Me versus the World

by

Killian O'Boyle

I ran faster and faster. He was watching me intensely from a distance. I can do it I thought, I can go faster. I ran the last 100 metres or so and finished exhausted. I panted as I caught my breath.

"That was great running." he said. "You really have a good stride. Have a Club Orange"

I gulped it down. He always had a Club Orange for me. It was great.

After the training we said goodbye till the following week. I jogged home.

"So how was the running?" my father asked.

"Yeah grand, great. Dave's a great coach.

He's really pushing me"

I was twelve.

Confirmation next year.

I was a bit goofy on account of my thumb sucking, but growing up into a pre- teen.

"That's great, come out and help me with the hedge."

I had a quick drink and spent the next hour collecting leaves as my old man clipped.

My friend from across the road walked over. "Here, do you want to play football?"

"Sure, but I have to do this first."

"OK, see you later."

It was a typical family road; thirty-three houses in a cul- de-sac. Close knit. Middle class. Nice neighbours. Normal. Safe.

The following week I was back running with Dave. Dave was older. A man. He offered to coach me as I was a good runner. Not great … but in the school team. Conor and Stephen ran with us too. We enjoyed it. First time I was pushed hard really. After training one night, Dave told me there was a race in Belfast coming up in a month. "We could go together."

He did it last year with another kid. It was great fun and we could stay in a hotel. He'd organise everything. It'd be good for my development to race against other kids. I was thrilled. "Mum, Dad, guess what?"

"What, darling?" my mother replied.

My father read the paper.

"Dave has organised for me to be entered in a race next month in Belfast. It'll be great. Can I go, can I?"

"Erm, well we'll think about it." said Mum.

"What do you mean? Why can't I go? It'd be good for my development as a runner." I whined.

Mum smiled. "I didn't say you *couldn't* go, I said we'd think about it."

"You're *not* going!" Dad interjected, sternly.

"Why not? For God's sake, you're so mean" I started to cry. Not getting my way for something so trivial yet so important at twelve. I stomped up the stairs, slammed my bedroom door, and flung myself on the bed.

"Bloody hell," I thought, "why are they so God damn unfair?"

I fell asleep.

I met Dave at the next training session.

"Well, are you allowed to come to Belfast?"

"No, my parents won't let me. I don't know why. I'm really sorry."

"Don't worry about it. Maybe next time you'll be lucky. Here … have a Club Orange."

My running sessions around the park with Dave petered out. The summer ended and I went back to school in September. It was confirmation year so a big year and my last in primary school.

9 months later, 1985

"Ok kids you're getting your confirmation

photos tomorrow. The photographer will be here all day to take the photos. Make sure you wear your confirmation outfit with your rosette and medal." Mr Leahy says. "And make sure you look your best; no picking your noses or scratching your arses!"

"Ha ha." the whole class sniggers.

Next day we're all dressed up in the confirmation outfits. There's navy blazers and grey pants, white shirts and black pants, hairs combed sideways, duck arsed, too long and thick. I have a special green and brown outfit. It's awful. It's the 1980s!

"Hey … O'Boyle … you wouldn't get into heaven in that outfit." Conor guffaws.

"Get lost. Here, are you taking the pledge?"

"Yeah, no drinking till we're eighteen," he says, "not sure what all the fuss is about. I tasted my old man's beer last weekend when he wasn't looking, just to know what I'm giving up. It was yuk, like stale bubbles! Hey did you see Mason has a pack of cigarettes in his bag? I saw him smoking them yesterday at the bus stop."

"Did you? He's only eleven!"

"I know! Shush he might hear."

Mason grumpily stares over. His straight bowl hairstyle framing his skinny freckled face. He wasn't pretty. I'd had a bust up with him before. Two bloody noses. We turn away from each other.

"I tried to smoke one once. I retched everywhere." I stammer.

"Here, what are you going to do with your confirmation money?" Robert asks.

"Don't know. Maybe get a 'Pac-Man' game. It's brilliant."

"Stephen's getting a Commodore 64. Much better than the Spectrum."

"Yeah, that's rubbish."

"You're rubbish."

"Ha ha!"

We're pushing and shoving in the line, down the hallway and into the gym area. The photographers have set up. They're wearing their suits and there's a big camera, two actually, and they have lights and those tinfoil things to reflect the light.

"What are they for?"

"Dunno, make you look like a film star maybe."

"They're not magicians!"

"Piss off."

"Right" says the photographer's assistant. "You're next."

In I go, up I sit. "Now look at the camera and smile."

"Oh look it's Dave." I say to myself as I recognise my old running coach. He's the photographer. He's all dressed up in his suit. Looks professional to me. So that's what he does. We don't acknowledge each other.

Photos are taken, there's a big flash.

"OK another one - look this way" says the assistant.

Another flash.

"Right, you're done. Next!"

I look back at Dave as I leave. He's busy getting ready for the next photo.

Later that evening, after school, at dinner with my sisters we're talking about our day. My sisters are in their pink ballet uniforms talking rubbish as per usual. Girls!!

"Hey Mum, guess what?" I speak up.

"What?"

"Dave was the confirmation photographer today. He took all the boys' photos. Funny."

"Who?"

"Dave, my running coach. You wouldn't let me go to Belfast with him last summer."

My father rattles his paper.

"Yes, darling." says Mum. "Maybe you should take off your confirmation outfit and go out and play on the road."

"OK, see you." I say as I pinch my sisters on the way out the door.

"Hey" they both shout angrily.

The photos are given out. I look goofy. My parents buy one. It goes on the wall. It doesn't last.

Sometime in 1991

"Killian."

"Yes Mum."

"Do you remember that guy you used to do the running with?"

"Yes"

"Well, I heard that he left his wife. Just walked out. Didn't come back."

"That's weird."

"Yes."

"Maybe it was just as well I wasn't allowed go to Belfast"

"I think maybe it was."

Dad rattles his paper in the next room.

Mistaken Identity

recalled by

Maureen Grainger

It was the 22nd of August 1942. I was just six years old and I was standing at my bedroom door, listening to the noise coming from the dining room, situated on the cool side of our bungalow, high up on stilts above the sugar cane at Carripuchima; Tate and Lyle's Sugar Estate in Trinidad.

My father was the Veterinary Surgeon there, and in charge of all the working animals - mostly mules and water buffaloes, and he and my mother were having a dinner party to which, not only was I not invited, but I was told to stay in my room 'like a good girl'.

I was furious.

I got out of bed and opened the door a little wider to hear the voices better, and was nearly caught by my father who came out into the corridor to answer the telephone.

He listened for a long time after the caller announced himself, but said very little in response other than 'Oh no ...oh no ... no ... no that's terrible.'

When he returned to the dining room there was a hush. Maybe it was the look on his face that quietened the guests. "The coyote's done for" he said, "I've just heard from someone who was there and saw it happen."

At that very moment my mother came out of the dining-room and started walking along the landing towards my bedroom. I carefully pulled the door shut and raced for my bed, just getting into it as she stuck her head round the door.

Happy I was asleep, she went back to the dining room from where, if I listened very carefully, I could just hear the guests talking about the coyote, and about how it had been 'done for'.

I tried my best to picture the poor creature ... wondering if she had babies waiting for her to return. Who would look after them? Coyotes are dangerous animals but they needn't be killed; they can simply be driven off. Nobody has the right to dismiss the life of a poor thing foraging for food for its young as if it was nothing. Even at six I knew that was wrong.

I lay awake for ages, thinking of the baby coyotes waiting for a mother that was never going to return. It was a big issue for me and one might have expected that the pitiful images of the animal's death would have prayed on my mind for days.

They didn't of course, for the next day was my birthday and I got a new bicycle - a red one with big wheels, and somehow the coyote got forgotten.

And then, one day some sixty years later, in 2002 or thereabouts, when Alan and I, on an all-day guided tour of Tobago, were settled on a sunny headland eating the excellent picnic lunch the Turtle

Beach Hotel had provided, I got an amazing surprise.

We had been listening to our tour guide giving us some interesting facts about the island and its history. For example, we had no idea that, rather astonishingly, it had once been a colony of Latvia! And that, during the fourteen, fifteen and sixteen hundreds, when many European countries were still colonising different far flung parts of the world, Tobago change hands thirty one times!

"As to more recent history," he went on, "let me tell you about the extraordinary story of a cargo ship that, driven onto those rocks down there by gunfire coming from a German submarine, was pounded to bits by the waves."

"The vessel," he told us, had been loaded with essential food and commercial goods necessary for the island's survival. It had come under gunfire when the submarine had been forced to the surface because of the shallowness of the water, and from there it opened up with its deck mounted gun, firing round after round into the stricken vessel that was eventually forced onto the rocks where it slowly disintegrated under the power of the sea.

"What happened to the ship's crew?" A man in our group asked.

"Saved. Every single one. They scrambled ashore and climbed over the rocks to safety."

"Extraordinary, so not a single man died?"

"I wish I could say none did." the guide replied. "But I'm afraid quite a few of the sub's crew perished. It had got so tied up in trying to sink the freighter that it had failed to spot a fast-approaching British warship until its shells came raining down."

"Wow ... so what happened then?"

"Panicking when the water all around started erupting, the U-boat began manoeuvring back to deeper water so it could dive and slip away."

"Ah ... so it escaped!"

"It tried to ... but the water was too shallow for a deep dive and it got stuck on the bottom, where it was an easy target for the depth charges the warship began lobbing onto it. It was also very vulnerable because, though those commanding the warship didn't know it, the U-Boat's controls had been damaged. It never had any real chance of escaping."

I pointed down to the waves crashing onto the rocks 50 feet below where we were sitting. "And this all happened right down there?" I asked.

He nodded. "It's hard to believe, I know. But I assure you it's true. A few German sailors did manage to get out of the U-boat and make it to the surface. They were the lucky ones for they wound up spending the rest of the war in a compound on the island. The others all drowned.

As the story slowly emerged, I began to see how I may have misinterpreted my father's words all those years ago and I held up a finger. "Do you happen to know what the ship that was lost down there was called?"

The guide nodded again. "Sure, everyone on this island knows her name; it's part of our history. She was called The Coyote."

The Dresses in My Life

by

Jillian Godsil

I remember the pink satin dress. It had a large bow at the back and I'd never worn anything so beautiful before. It belonged to someone else of course – 'preloved' as it's called today or 'sustainable fashion'.

I wore the dress, a dusky pink, one Sunday. I've no idea who pre-loved it but I see myself, as a photograph standing in front of the French doors in the garden.

There is a photograph indeed of my mother and my two eldest siblings in a similar pose. We must have chosen that spot as a family for official photographs. The home of my childhood, the home where I was born in fact, at a time when home births were a norm rather than a considered choice.

Did I mention I was born by hypnosis at home some six years before I wore my pink dress and was photographed for the joy in my memory. No, that was not the norm.

Our neighbours around the time of my pink dress installed a swimming pool in their back garden. A gigantic effort resulting in a long rectangular pool swathed in blue plastic liner that was held down by coloured concrete paving stones around the edge. It took up most of the garden.

As a family we helped the build and so could use the pool. Never on our own, but once our neighbours were in the water, we all rushed to find our swimming togs and jumped in too, regardless of the weather.

Once, the older boy next door released live eels he had caught the day before into the pool. They swam like demented serpents hemmed in the rectangular prison with their strong bodies threshing up and down the length of the pool. For days they ruled the water, and the pool was out of bounds. Their end was horrific. The same boy fished them out with a string net and decapitated them with a large kitchen knife. No went into the pool for some time after that.

That family sold the house and moved away. A new family with small grandchildren arrived and a chance falling into the pool of one such child caused the pool to be filled in that summer.

There is another dress I remember well too, a stripey summer one, quite new. It was very pretty but then I was sixteen, everything is pretty when you are sixteen. I was in Cork for my long summer holidays and my brother, my aunt and I went to a local church to watch a wedding. The mother of the bride spoke with my aunt and invited us to the dancing part of the wedding party, held in a big farm building cleared out for the occasion. I loved it and invited every male up to dance- regardless of age.

For my school debs I invested in designer clothing, a Frank Usher black jersey pantsuit. It was different but I loved it. I wore it at several Trinity Balls and aside from one cigarette burn on my sleeve – from a reckless dancer on the dance floor not me – it is still perfect. How do I know? I never gave it away or threw it out. It's with my wedding dress in an antic, not mine, a friend's, as I don't currently have an attic.

One Trinity Ball I decided to have a dress made. A seamstress with inexpensive charges did the honours but, in my ignorance, I chose an ugly pattern and unsuitable material. The end result was not what I wanted but I was twenty one.

During my long farm holidays, I had been told before by over-generous country folk, that I would look good in a black bin liner! This dress, through no fault of the dress maker, resembled a dark blue sparkly bin liner. I don't think I looked that good in that. Maybe they were telling lies.

My wedding dress was also pink, just above the knee, with a pink chiffon scarf reminiscent of Isadora Duncan, or so I thought. I was married on Valentine's Day on a Fijian Island. What a day to remember, or to forget as I am now divorced. It was a pretty dress even though I am not sure pink is my colour.

I have two children and at both their christenings I put them into the same, saved christening robe – but I too wore the same outfit, identical down to a dashing black straw hat. I was rather proud of that – me fitting into the same outfit, not my children fitting into the robe. I asked my husband repeatedly on the second christening to take a picture so we could frame the two images side by side – in those days we did not have camera phones - but he forgot. That is a shame to my mind.

So many pretty dresses over the years.

During two years of COVID I have worn nothing but active wear and hoodies. Every so often,

I peer into my wardrobe, the tall skinny one in the corner of my bedroom, next to the bedside table, and when I open the door there appears a riot of colour that would out-blossom a prize-winning flower bed. I almost need sunglasses such is the dazzle. When lockdown finishes, I want to make memories again with these dresses, if they still fit.

Starting at School

by

Susie Knight

I was four years old when I went to a small private school in the village. The school was run by a teacher called Miss Swann. She lived in an old Georgian house that had outbuildings with large wooden doors with metal latches and stone floors. These outbuildings had possibly been stabling or a dairy or maybe a wash house. This was the school room.

There was a blackboard and easel and little low tables with ink wells. There were about eight children in the school, but all were boys except me. I can still remember most of their names. There was Pip and Paul Barnes, they were twins and belonged to the vicar who lived next-door to the school. Then there was

Christopher Sharp, Anthony McClennan, John Saddler, Michael Sullivan, Martin Hoare and me.

Miss Swann seemed quite old to me as a four-year-old, so she could have been anything from forty to eighty! She did have white hair, so that may put her in the older bracket. She was a jolly woman and believed in fresh air. She took us out into the meadow at the back of the house and showed us things like catkins, which she said were sometimes called lambs' tails and explained other aspects of nature. She read us stories from the Enid Blyton book of Nature. A great book which I found and bought in a second-hand book shop many years later. I have passed it on to my Grandchildren now. They love the stories too!

When we were in the meadow, we were allowed to run about and play. I remember playing horses on my own. Galloping around the field pretending to be Black Beauty and neighing in the wind. The boys tended to play war games and I was rarely included.

In the winter we were given warm milk to drink and had Rich Tea biscuits to eat. I still like those biscuits. They are comforting. Once Miss Swann told me off for playing with money spiders on my desk.

Once a week we were allowed to go into the big house and up the stairs to the sitting room. It was a small, lovely room with a view of the clock tower. Miss Swann had a piano in this room, and we were taught to sing the National Anthem, Away in a Manger, The First Nowell and A Froggy Would A Wooing Go!

My Granny used to come and collect me at about one o'clock and on the way home she would take me into the sweet shop and buy me a Cadbury's Five Boy Bar. Then I would tell her all about my day and all the things the boys had done!

When it got to my fifth birthday, I had all the boys at my birthday party. We had rich tea biscuits with pink icing on and my Mum made toffee apples, but the toffee didn't set!

So, we had our apples on sticks accompanied by soft toffee on a spoon.

I still have the handwritten reports from Miss Swann. It was a lovely entry into school life, but the following year we all went to big school!

Big School

I was taken to a classroom and told that my teacher was called Mrs Howell. I was told to sit on a little chair opposite a girl called Carol. She had a lovely smile, but all her teeth were completely black!

Carol's family came from Caersws in Wales. We became good friends, and she taught me how to say the very long Welsh station, which I can still say today, in a very 'English' kind of a way!

Llanfairpwllgwyngyllgogerychwyrndrobwllllantysiliogogogoch

When we had all been allocated a desk and had been registered, we were lined up and taken to the Hall. There were so many children, all in lines. Big children at the back and us right at the front. It was very different from Miss Swan's school.

Mr Thomas was the head of music and he particularly admired Jacqueline du Pré. He told us about her and played a recording of her playing Elgar's Cello Concerto. It was the first piece of classical music that I had heard. It will always stay with me.

He taught us to sing hymns but also songs like 'On Ilkla Moor Baht'at , Nelly Bligh, Molly Malone and Bony was a Warrior.

Mr Thomas also took us on a school trip to The Annual Children's Concert at The Royal Festival Hall, in London. It was a magical and memorable experience.

The village where I lived was in East London and on the Thames. During the Second World War, it had been badly hit by bombs heading for London. The air raid shelters were still in the playground of the school. They were dark and smelly. I couldn't imagine having to go in them for lessons! One day the fire bell rang, and we all had to go to the front of the school.

An unexploded bomb had been found in the field behind the school. The bomb disposal unit arrived, and all the children were sent home.

I don't remember hearing the explosion, but the windows of the assembly hall were blown out! If I recollect correctly, the bomb was deactivated but there was a controlled explosion.

When I was a little older, probably about nine, I had a teacher called Mr Nobbs. An unfortunate name for a teacher! He was very good at Arts and Crafts and got us to make string-holders out of coconuts. The best bit was making the hole in the coconut and drinking the milk!

Ah … Happy Days!

Belfast

by

Killian O'Boyle

Tick, Tick, Tick.
Tick, Tick, Tick.

My mother looks at her watch. She waits at home on Stranmillis Road. She's seven months pregnant. She struggles to get up. Outside it's quiet enough. It's a middle-class Protestant area. There were riots last night. In the distance from their bedroom my parents could hear the commotion. The flicker of burning cars was visible from their window. It was early in December 1972.

There was a distant explosion. There were gunshots. They lay on their bed listening. Dad suggested they get under the bed in case 'rick o shea' came through the window!

'OK" Mum said, forgetting about her 'condition'. She struggled off the bed. Once down, getting under the bed became an obvious impossibility. They laughed. They sighed. Dad pulled the covers over them. They fell asleep to the sounds of 'The Troubles' echoing throughout the city …lost, alone, and in murderous turmoil.

Colm (Dad) phoned.

'Hi Cacks" he cheerfully chirped down the phone. "What you doing?"

"Not a lot to be honest"

"Well, I am doing a few Christmas bottle deliveries this afternoon. Would you like to come with me?"

"Alright … yes…I suppose so."

"OK, I will pick you up at two o'clock."

"Good … see you later"

***

'James Martin' was up from Derry. He was just 21 but a determined and dedicated freedom fighter. He was in a warehouse off the Falls Road. He and two others were putting the car bomb together. The charge was big. The alarm clock timer they used was dangerous, fragile and could blow the three of them to hell.

Martin walks behind the car as he checks the work. He goes outside after the bomb is completed, jumps into his brown Capri, then checks the glove compartment for his revolver. He takes out a cigarette, strikes a Friendly match, lights the fag, takes a deep drag and as he exhales the grey smoke relaxes him into the seat. He's ready for tonight. Death may come to some but the war is raging. He pulls the car out and drives off.

***

"Right" says Dad, helping Mum into the car.

"I have 4 bottles to drop. I have Stevie Adams on the Omagh Road., then Peter Bates, Paul

O'Connor and finally we'll go back into town for Charles Latham in the book publishers."

Dad was running a waste paper plant in Belfast. He'd been sent up from Dublin to try and make it profitable. Money wasn't being made. It was in the middle of a war zone. He knew the score. The city was a mess.

Only the previous week he'd given one of the plant workers a lift home.

"There's going to be trouble tonight, Mr O'Boyle." Paddy said.

Paddy hadn't shown for work since. He never would again. But it was Christmas time and Dad knew the value of human contact in business - relationships were the lifeblood of commercial life. A cup of tea, a dram of whiskey. Time chatting was the way you built a long-term client. So off we went; Dad, Mum and unborn me.

Dad took his time normally, but knowing Mum wanted company and had come along for the drive, he was diplomatic in turning down the invitations for a drink. They pulled up to the last call. Mum said she was tired and asked him to make this one quick.

Dad got out of the car. "OK love" he said "just 5 minutes"

Mum opened her magazine. She'd already read it. She looked down. Her feet were swollen, she needed a pee, I gave her a kick. "OK baby" she said, "quieten down in there". It was darkening now. 5 pm. She checked her watch:

Tick, Tick, Tick

She wiggled her toes. She adjusted the rear-view mirror. She looked tired. She noticed a tall gangly man getting out of the car behind her. He was young with curly hair and wore a brown wool jumper with a darkened jacket. He had a stoop. He walked by and on up the street. He was smoking a cigarette.

"Where is Colm?"

In the publishers, Charles accepted the Whiskey graciously.

He liked Colm. He was a southern Catholic. Not like the ones up here.

"Will you not have a glass with me?" he asked.

"I won't." said Dad. "I have Kathryn in the car. She's 8 months pregnant."

"Is she indeed. Well, that'll make it an interesting January."

"It will. I better dash. Happy Christmas to you and the family."

"Happy Christmas Colm." Charles replied.

Dad ran down the stairs. When he got into the car Mum jumped slightly as she had nodded off against the window. There was condensation on the windscreen. Dad wiped it off with a rag. He started the engine and reversed a bit too quickly. He bumped into a car behind.

"Damn, that car wasn't there when I parked" he said. He hadn't seen it with the fogged up back window. It was only a small tip so he wasn't inclined to put a note on the car. He indicated to pull out and then lost the engine in the gear change.

"Bloody hell!"

He turned the ignition again.

"Right, we're off love."

Tick, Tick, Tick.

Mum looked at her watch. Dinner time. Maybe eggs and chips tonight. She wasn't in the mood for cooking

Tick, Tick, Tick.

The alarm went off, the fuse ignited. There was a crack and then the explosion.

The bomb blew the car up and shards of glass and metal flew through the air. The store beside was all smashed up. The blast tore through the shop and took out four cars.

Dad slammed on the brakes. The car parked behind them a few seconds ago was all aflame.

My mother shrieked in fright.

Dad looked around - there was no one on the streets. An alarm was going off. I kicked again in my mother's womb.

"Are you OK love?"

"Yes, but can we go home?"

"Sure we can."

I was born 8 weeks later.

Bedsit Blues

by

Pat Mullan

No one moved, all eyes were glued to the television. As the new boy, and the youngest on the block, I was obviously expected to get up and answer the door after there'd been a third loud rap on the knocker.

Two black men stood there; arms folded. In their forties. Wrangler bell bottoms and matching bright acrylic tee shirts, rocking backwards and forward on their sockless sandaled feet.

Nothing at St. Columb's had in any way prepared me for this.

"Just who do you think you are, Punk?" asked

the taller of the two, the one with the curly sideburns and bushy moustache who had a big gold medallion hanging around his neck. "This is *our* street," he said, pushing me back against the door, his right hand gripping me around my throat. "And if you, or any of those other funky dudes inside ever, and I mean ever, lift a finger against any of the kids in this street, you'll have me and Success here to answer to. And we won't be so polite if there is a next time."

Success stood six foot five and at least sixteen stone, a look of contempt in his eyes.

He spat abundantly at my feet. "You hear that, boy?" he asked.

"I'm sorry Mister," I replied, as I reached up to ease the pressure on my throat, "but we were just watching the soccer and some young lads threw pebbles at the window. We just warned them off, that's all."

"You think you can come here and lay down the law to us and tell our kids what they can or can't do? This is our street, just remember that."

He removed his hand from my throat and brushed and unruffled the cheese-cloth shirt that I'd picked up at the Petticoat Lane market the previous Sunday.

I could just see the butt of the revolver protruding from Success's left side pocket as the two visitors made their way down the front steps and on to the street.

A bunch of twenty odd black kids noisily surrounded them as they walked away.

We were the only white "family" on Landstake Road in Shepherd's Bush, London. Two double beds, a single camping bed, a foam mattress, a sink, a small fridge, a two-ringed gas cooker with grill but no oven. A table and four rigid institutional waiting room chairs in front of the window and that was the extent of the furniture. A colour poster of Rory Gallagher dominated the room. A lino-covered bedsit that accommodated twelve of us, six working night shift on the London Underground doing track maintenance, the rest of us working as many days as we could get for a British Rail sub-contractor. All summer jobs.

A heady mix of mouldering lard, sweaty feet and damp permeated the room day and night.

Clothes and working boots everywhere.

The rodent footprints on the solidified lard in the frying pan shocked me at first but, after a week, like the rest, I paid no heed and fried up the breakfast with impunity. The communal record player, bought along with a few dozen LPs as a job lot in the second-hand record shop on Goldhawk Road was seldom off, except at times like this when there was a soccer match on the television. The second half was just beginning when I'd got up to answer the door. We all thought it was the young bloody kids again, not more than nine or ten, the ones who had been throwing small pebbles and bits of debris at our window from the street below earlier, during the rigged mid-afternoon West Germany versus Austria game in the 1982 World Cup.

It was my turn to run the youngsters this time. Weak at the knees, heart pounding from the threatening incident at the door, I went back inside and opened the one to the bed-sit.

There was pandemonium.

Northern Ireland were after scoring and were one goal to nil up against Spain in Valencia. I had just missed Gerry Armstrong scoring the goal that brought Northern Ireland into the World Cup second round.

The Attic

by

Chris Struelens

Thinking about my childhood always takes me back to the time when we as a family lived with my grandmother. The house and garden were large. We could wander through the basement kitchens, then go one floor up to our family's living space, and another floor up to our bedrooms. My grandmother's rooms and living room were off limits to my brother and me.

Outside the bedrooms there was a large landing where we also had a nice play area. But it didn't stop there. In the ceiling of the landing was a hatch that gave access to the attic and, every spring according to my grandmother, it was time to clean it.

My father would be ordered to raise the ladder; the hatch would be opened and the adventure could begin. We would watch and wait for my father to open the hatch and let us crawl up. My mother and grandmother were at the bottom of the ladder and did not go up with us. They shouted that we had to be careful and thought it was irresponsible of my father to let us up, as if we were going and climbing a mountain. After an exciting climb we would reach the attic and the magic could then begin.

The attic was a beautiful space ... completely floored and with thick beams and two dormer windows we could not see out, because they were too high. But that was not all, the magic mainly consisted of what was *in* the attic.

Actually, it was not so much: an old chair, an old grandfather clock as in the fairy tale of the wolf and the seven goats, forgotten books, a chest of junk and another chest in which were my father's army clothes dating from his military service. It contained army shirts, army vests, boots and trousers. Also, there were two berets which my brother and I put on our heads. Dad put on his soldier's uniform top, hoisted the brush to rest on his shoulder and, so dressed, we paraded across the attic. Obviously, there hadn't been much clearing out done in that house for a longtime. I was particularly fascinated by a huge pram with a porcelain push bar that we found up there, but I was too small to push it so my brother helped me, and we wheeled it all around the attic floor while my father removed the cobwebs.

After a while, according to my father, the attic was tidy enough and it was time to start the descent back down into the house. The hatch would be closed again and the attic would not be entered for another year, until the following spring probably.

What happened to all that stuff in the attic? Where is it now? I have no idea other than that the military uniforms were taken back by the army once my father had passed the call-up age and he could no longer be re-enlisted.

The berets didn't have to go back, I think my brother still has them.

The clock is at my daughter's house in Ireland,

And the pram is in our living room showing off my Teddy Bear and a few dolls I have kept for the next generation; family mementos, each with a story from days gone by.

Dr Who Terror

by

Mary Cait Hermon

Like most children of the seventies, I grew up watching Dr Who on a Saturday evening. Probably, also like most children of that era, it frightened the pants off me most weeks. Apologies to those of you reading this who may never have watched Dr Who, but it was a classic, in fact, it's still running on television today and my nephew is still hooked at the age of 21!

Briefly – just in case you are not a fan – Doctor Who is a science fiction series which has been on air since the early 1960's. It follows the adventures of a "Time Lord" called The Doctor, who is very human in every way, apart from the fact that he is hundreds of years old and never dies, he just "regenerates". At every regeneration, a new version of The Doctor appears, but that always happens at the end of a series and you have to wait on tenterhooks until the start of the next series to see how he will look in his new form. In my day, he was invariably mortally wounded in the season finale and you would see the beginning of the regeneration process, but then the credits would roll before it was complete. (This usually happened when the actor playing him wanted to do something else with their life and a new actor had to be inserted.) It never bothers anybody when we have a Regeneration, in fact it is just as exciting as finding out who the new Bond actor will be when the current guy gets too old to play the role. This excitement still continues at every Regeneration today, with the current Doctor being played by a woman, which would have been unheard of back in the 60's!

In my era, our Doctor was played by the actor

John Pertwee, who went on to become Worzel Gummage afterwards (if you don't know who that is, you'll just have to Google it, as I don't have the space to explain that one!)

Anyway, The Doctor travels the universe in a box called the TARDIS. TARDIS stands for Time and Relative Dimension in Space and it's a machine that travels around in time, materialising and dematerialising in and out of every adventure. The most exciting thing about it is that it is huge inside, with lots of rooms, but looks very much smaller on the outside. When The Doctor first travelled in it, there was a gadget called the Chameleon Circuit on board which could make the TARDIS transform to look like an object that was common for the time or planet he had arrived at, thereby hiding it in plain sight. However, it lost this ability due to a malfunction at some point, after that it always looked like a blue British police box, which, apparently, was a common sight in Britain back in the 60's.

The Doctor travels with a companion – these

companions also change regularly series by series – and together they fight for good, try to save civilisations (alien and human) and help people or worlds in need. My favourite companion was his small robotic dog, which was called K9. It all sounds like a great and heroic story of bravery and derring do, but there are also aliens and monsters. To my young eyes, these creatures were absolutely terrifying, but I can't really describe what they looked like as I was too scared to actually look at the screen when they were on.

Back in the 70's, his worst enemies by far were the Daleks. These were very jazzy looking metal bins with a sort of periscope thing and skinny arms. They rolled around on wheels and said in mechanical voices things like "o-bey the dah-leks, o-bey the dah-leks" and "ex-ter-min-ate, ext-ter-min-ate".

I can see now, on reading that last bit, that they don't sound too scary by modern standards, but believe you me, when I was a child, they were the scariest monsters ever invented.

Now that I have set the scene of that fateful summer evening, back to my own terrifying tale.

In our house, we watched Dr Who religiously every week with our parents. Saturday evening would see the sofa pulled out from the wall so that my two sisters and I could hide behind it to watch. We peered over the back of the sofa and dived to the floor for the scary bits. As soon as we even suspected the Daleks might appear, we flung ourselves to safety flat on our stomachs. My mother always watched from behind a cushion or with her eyes shut. My father would sit back and laugh at how ridiculous we all were. We all loved this show, but we children were also terrified by it.

One Saturday evening, I was probably about 6 or 7, there we were behind the sofa as usual, my mother watching The Doctor's adventures with her eyes closed, when my father walked into the room. Luckily the episode we were watching was just finishing, when he announced that there was a monster in the greenhouse. Well, we nearly crawled under the sofa altogether at that point.

"Come on," he said, "we'll have to catch it!"

We were terrified. A monster in our garden? Was it an alien? Worse, was it a Dalek??? And hold on a second there now, had he just said "catch it"??!! Was he completely mad? I looked at Mum, as she stared at him in shock, which made me even more certain that Dad had obviously been mind-zapped by aliens from Dr Who while he was picking the tomatoes for our dinner.

To my horror, Mum agreed that we should most certainly be ridding ourselves of any monster who was planning to take up residence in our greenhouse, and what's more, we should do it straight away. With great trepidation, we went to the back door, pulled on our wellies and followed Dad down the side of the shed and up to the greenhouse door, pulling Mum along with us for moral support.

Our greenhouse back then was like another

world to me. I rarely went in, but when I did, it was like being on another planet. The green plants (presumably tomatoes and runner beans) climbed the walls either side of a central concrete pathway and formed a green tunnel overhead, brushing your arms as you walked past. When you entered the door, you had to climb over a low block wall and then you were at the lower level. I can't remember exactly what was at this level, but I do remember that you turned right and went up a couple of steps to the main event.

The air was always hot and moist compared to the outside. I used to believe this was what it must feel like in a tropical jungle, but I was always slightly worried about Triffids too (another alien life form, but not from Dr Who!), which is why I rarely went in alone.

Dad stood at the doorway to the greenhouse and urged us inside and onwards towards whatever lay in wait for us. We crept through the entrance and slowly, clutching and shoving each other, we made our way up the steps and along the path. Our eyes were as big as saucers and swivelled from side to side as we progressed, ready to flee at the first sign of anything moving. Mum and Dad waited at the lower level, watching our journey.

I'm not sure why we didn't worry that they were letting us catch the monster on our own. They seemed happy to wait and see whether we were sucked up into an alien light beam which would transport us to a spaceship and away into the ether, possibly for ever.

We reached the end of the path but we found no monster. I can't remember if we felt relieved or disappointed, but we turned back and looked down the long green tunnel towards our parents.

"Down this way, quick, I think it's an alien!" Dad exclaimed, as he beckoned us back the way we had come. We swiftly retreated towards the safety of our loving, caring, protective (hmmm!) parents. Dad pointed down to the ground near where they stood. We crept closer to see what he was showing us.

A box. A long strong looking cardboard one

lying on its side with the flap of one end resting on some straw that was poking out of it. The fact that it was so long, and on its side, meant we'd be unable to see what was lurking in it from a safe distance. We would have to get right down onto our hands and knees if we wanted to catch even a glimpse of the alien that was in there, and we weren't too sure if this would be a good idea or not. Dr Who's aliens were loud and obvious, *they* didn't lurk in the shadows of cardboard boxes in your greenhouse.

"Watch this," said Dad.

He held a lettuce leaf to the opening of the box, there was a sudden movement from inside, the leaf was snatched from his hand and disappeared into the black depths of the box. We shrieked in fright. Now we were in a dilemma. The box was between us and our parents – what should we do?? Would the alien snatch us as we tried to pass and eat us up too? Mum waved us towards her and we made a run for it, leaping past the open front of the box and into her waiting arms.

Dad picked another lettuce leaf and held it out to us, "Go on, you have a go!" It took a while and a lot of cajoling and encouragement, but eventually my eldest sister, who was always very brave, took the leaf and slowly bent down to hold it to the opening. Again, a sudden movement and the leaf disappeared into the box. Honestly, at that point we may all have wet our knickers in fright! This was the most terrifyingly exciting thing ever to happen to us and we couldn't contain ourselves.

Dad held out another lettuce leaf, this time to my next sister, who got the same response from whatever was inside the box. Then it was my turn. With shaking hands, I took the leaf from my father and, with Mum holding my other hand, I reached out towards the box. I could hear a noise from within, and snatched my hand back, convinced it would be bitten off, or, worse, I would be pulled into the black depths of the cavernous TARDIS-like space that the box had become.

"Go on," said Dad, "you'll be fine, just go a

bit closer….."

I pulled my mother with me and scooted a teeny-weeny bit closer, then I once again reached out with the leaf. I managed to get the very tip of it just inside the edge of the box. Bam!!! It was gone in a flash and I fell back onto my bottom in shock.

I looked up at my sisters. We couldn't believe it. A real, live, genuine alien in our greenhouse! We each had another go at the lettuce experiment and each time with the same result, this was thrilling!

"Can we keep it? Pleeeeeeease!" We pleaded with our parents. How cool would it be to have a pet alien? Nobody else had one, we'd have friends queueing up to come to our house. Maybe we could even charge them to feed the alien lettuce leaves.

"We'll see." That was as close as we ever got when we asked for a new pet. It meant neither "yes of course" nor "absolutely not". I now know that this is the standard response for parents who don't want to agree to something, but don't want to let their children down immediately either. "We'll see" nearly always ends up as a "No" in the end.

"You'll have to take it out and show it to them. They might not like how it looks," said my mother to my father. We were very nervous about this suggestion. An alien that you couldn't see, hidden in a box was something we could handle. Seeing it in real life was quite another thing.

We pulled back into our mother's arms as Dad knelt down before the dark black opening and reached into the box. Almost at once he fell backwards towards us, "Dammit, it bit me!"

He clutched his hand close to his chest. Now what would happen? Would he turn into a slimy green alien with red dripping eyes and skin covered in bursting, oozing boils?

No. He wiped his hand on his jeans and knelt back in front of the box ... took a deep breath and, once again, reached inside. After straining and grunting, and a few muttered oaths, he pulled something out that writhed and wriggled as it tried to free itself from his grip. We all screamed and hid our faces in Mum's chest, we couldn't look for fear of what we might see.

"It's OK, girls, you can look, it's not that bad," Mum soothed us. She urged us to turn and face the alien in Dad's arms. Eventually we plucked up the courage to peep over towards him out of the very corner of our eyes. We were stunned by what we saw - and even more desperate to be allowed to keep the thing he was now holding.

There, in his lap as he sat on the top step, was an enormous......black rabbit!

He had found it on the road and brought it home until the owner could be located. After much pleading, my parents agreed that we could keep the rabbit, but only if the owner could not be found.

We had to leave it in the greenhouse so that the dogs couldn't get at it, but this was not the best plan. A rabbit in a greenhouse? You can imagine that for that black furry creature, it was Mardi Gras every day, but after only one day Mum was looking up recipes for rabbit stew!

Luckily for the rabbit, the owner was located after only a few days and our plans of being firstly cool alien owners and then fluffy black rabbit owners came to an end. I don't think we even had time to tell any of our friends about our new pet before it went back from whence it came.

It just goes to show though, a bit of imagination at an impressionable age can leave you with a memory that lasts a lifetime!

Summer in West Cork

by

Bridget Aylmer

Combine harvesters are busy saving the crops –
the sun is shining and everything in the
Countryside is glistening. Having lived for the last 11
months in suburbia, seeing green fields with cattle
and sheep is a welcome sight. The freshness of the
country air and the freedom of space is exhilarating.
Memories flood back from Childhood Summers in
Castletownshend to the present day.

Way back in the 60s and early 70s, all our
holidays were spent on my grandparents' farm. My
grandfather had milking cows, store cattle and crops
of hay, corn and barley. It was traditional for the local

farmers to help each other with the harvesting. I always enjoyed the threshing as it meant porter for the men and lemonade for the women and children. My grandmother always laid on a big spread: large hams with potatoes and salad, apple tart with cream (all unpasturised), and great pots of strong tea. The regular workmen ate in the parlour or in the kitchen area on benches. The farmers and friends ate in the dining room. As children, we always enjoyed helping at this event.

Otherwise, our holiday time was spent in rowing boats, sailing boats, swimming, barbeques and getting up to mischief. We were like the Swallows and Amazons. Tremendous freedom. We watched meteor showers at what was fondly known as the bathing cove.

My aunt and uncle lived in a Castle which they ran as a guesthouse and, when we were teenagers, we were allowed to use the Sitting room in the West Tower for parties. Amongst our many friends were musicians, sculptors, visitors from the UK and America. An eclectic mix of young people. The sailing club ran a fancy-dress race called The Ancient Britain Race, though in name only. We dressed up on one occasion as 'The Boston Tea Party' and won a prize! Treasure Hunts were popular too and were held at The Red House.

Once we had a Game of Smugglers and Coastguards – the event was so convincing that the locals called the Gardai!

Tennis parties were also popular; where, in the mixed doubles, partners were arranged with the view of getting a beau.

Life moved on and, despite being in my early 20s, I still continued to visit Castletownshend for the sailing.

My first serious boyfriend was an art restorer and we met at one of the many parties held during the Summer of 1978 – a tall sallow handsome young man from Gloucestershire. He gave me a wonderful introduction to the art world and indeed the wider world. We are still friends to this day. In fact, he introduced me to my husband.

Life moves on though, and I have two sons. The elder son is married and has 2 children so I am a grandmother now. They all adore Castletownshend and spend a lot of time there.

My marriage broke up in 1993 and I have had several paramours. Now I am solo but I have many good men friends. I have met swarthy sailors, property investors, swindlers, teachers and, more recently, an artist with a colourful background; a fascinating man from Kerry who has travelled the world. Originally a draughtsman he then, in turn, became a statistician, a teacher and an artist.

Castletownshend (affectionately known to me as 'CT') has, and I believe always will, give me the peace of mind, the comfort and the freedom that I need to relax in this very busy world.

The Conscript

by

Alan Grainger

'God Helps Those Who Help Themselves'

said the beautifully lettered black text on the draped
and heavily tasselled pale blue banner painted in
furls over the fireplace.

Underneath someone had chalked

But let God help any man found helping himself in here

*

The room was high and airy, with double
bunk beds running the length of it either side of a
wide passage to the door. There was no carpet,

nothing to cover the well-worn floorboards, or hide the battered furniture standing on it dimly lit by a shaft of moonlight. Anyone still awake, had they looked out of the tall sash windows, would have seen rows of similar buildings stretching way back into the darkness.

Between the bunks, tall old narrow lockers were flanked by rifle stands bearing weapons, while on them, lying uncomfortably on their mattresses, forty bodies tossed and turned as they tried to get to sleep; forty brand new 'barely out of the box' soldiers, and I was one of them.

I was seventeen years old and still at school when I got my calling up papers and, within a couple of weeks, as a new 'barely eighteen year old' conscript, I was struggling to adjust to a military life in the old Cavalry Barracks in Colchester in South East England.

Not that it had been any great surprise; I'd always known I'd be conscripted like everybody else as soon as I was eighteen. My last years at school had been wonderful but, with enlistment hanging over my head, I couldn't focus on any thought of college or career. I was no different to the rest I suppose, none of us were able to concentrate on exams. High Wycombe Royal Grammar School had been good for me and I'd enjoyed my four years as a student there. True the staff members were old and infirm, or poor in health due to war injury or bad luck as I've mentioned, and quite a few were women - not the most effective for discipline in a boy's school, but I'd enjoyed it all. I'd done well in my class and exam work, I was a sergeant in The Corps, and I played rugby for the school. Yes, all in all, a good time.

Now it was different though, now I was a soldier; a raw recruit, lined up and ready to be fashioned into a fighting machine, and I lay on my back staring at the cracked barrack-room ceiling, wondering how I'd get on in my new life.

I'd met up with two school friends at

Liverpool Street station that morning, Andy and Becky. Being of an age, we'd all received our enlistment call on the same day and all told to report to Cavalry Barracks, Colchester, sometime before six p.m. on the 26th of that month, They were both at Liverpool Station before me and looking for the Colchester platform, as were dozens and dozens of others clearly on the same mission for every single one was carrying his overnight gear in a paper carrier bag as instructed. A sergeant was standing at the barrier and hurrying everyone on to the waiting train. He glanced at our travel warrants and herded us through.

It's not far, Colchester, and we were soon stepping down onto a platform where another group of NCO's (non-commissioned officers) herded us out through a side gate into a fleet of canvas topped three ton lorries in which we were trundled through the town to the barracks. When we got there, we didn't even have enough time to note the starkness of the granite two storey buildings before the truck backed us up to one of them and we all climbed out, filed through a door, and entered a room in which there were four or five barber's chairs. One was vacant and a corporal, pointing to it, yelled 'Next. Come on, step on it boy, we haven't got all day.'

I went over and sat down, but before I had time to gather my thoughts the barber was giving me a 'Short back and Sides' so short I thought I'd been scalped. From there I was directed to the uniform store, where I was issued with freshly laundered but pretty ancient fatigues, a new pair of boots, a towel, and a small block of Lifebuoy disinfectant soap ... before being raced to a shower room where I was instructed to 'Get on with it' ... I did.

Once clear of the shower, I joined the other few dozen which included Andy and Becky; from each of whom exuded a powerful stench of carbolic as they milled around waiting to be allocated a room and a bed. We managed to stick together, and grabbed three adjacent top bunks in Room 26B then waited to see what would happen. It wasn't long before we found out.

A small man wearing a smartly pressed uniform and dazzling boots stamped into the room and bellowed for silence. 'Listen up,' he said, 'I'm Corporal Boot, 'Duke O'Wellington's Regiment. Right? You will do as I say. Right? Nah then you've got yer bunks. Right? Grab yourself three pally arses, and take 'em down the stable below and fill 'em with straw; them's yer mattresses. Right? I'll be back in ten minutes and I want you all back and finished by then, and we'll go for our supper. Right? Come on speak up are yer deaf or what? Right?'

We stood there mesmerized. Were we going to find ourselves in the Duke of Wellington's Regiment under this man who had a language of his own? The palliasses were about two foot six square, and four inches thick when stuffed, but they soon settled down to be about two and a half inches thick after a couple of nights on them. They were made out of heavy brown canvas and were sometimes referred to as 'biscuits', though I couldn't see why. By the time we got back to our room, sheets and pillowcases had been deposited on the end of each bunk.

'Five minutes.' yelled Corporal Boot, reappearing at the door and whacking it with his swagger stick. 'Five minutes 'n I want you fell in outside ready for the mess hall; we'll collect yer cutlery, plates, and mugs, on the way. Right? God Ormighty I've got a right lot 'ere, a right lot ... and just six weeks to bloody turn the lot of yers inter bloody soldiers ... God Ormighty.'

When we eventually got down to the mess hall, there was quite a long queue for us to join. We lined up at the back of it trying to look ahead and see what sort of grub was being dished up. Didn't look too bad - cottage pie or fish and chips. Once we'd collected our meal, we were told to fill up any unoccupied spaces on the wooden forms that flanked the long scrubbed wooden tables.

In the middle of each table, stacks of sliced bread towered over bowls of sugar, dishes of jam, and slabs of butter; all crudely presented but more than enough for everyone. Not that you'd think so, for the old hands who'd mixed in amongst us new recruits leaned across the table and, stabbing with their forks, captured as many slices of bread as they could, while at the same time knifing great lumps of butter and spoonsful of jam onto their plates. It was an astonishing sight, and it soon became apparent to me that 'self-service' meant 'self-serving'. The tea was in a bucket; it had the milk already in it and was doctored, so we were laughingly told by the older hands, with a substance to suppress our sexual instincts. We scooped out a mug full each as the bucket came round the table. The din of two hundred or more soldiers all talking at the same time was deafening, we could hardly hear ourselves think. After 'tea' we were finished for the day and filtered back to our barrack room where we sat around nervously whispering to each other. It had been shock treatment all day long and our heads were reeling with thoughts of home, and fear of the future. Day

One of our military careers was over.

On the bunk beneath me was a chap who'd just come out of Wormwood Scrubs prison. He'd 'done' three months for refusing to go down the mines (one in ten of all conscripts at that time were sent to serve down the coal mines instead of going into the fighting forces). I didn't blame him I'd have refused myself if my name had come out of the hat.

The chap under Becky was 'half gypsy' and had been a wall of death rider at a fairground, while the lad under Andy had been at Eton. The beds were desperately uncomfortable, and we tossed and turned all night long only finally getting off to sleep as the first streaks of daylight came filtering through the high sash windows.

'If things don't alter they'll stay as they are ... right?' boomed Corporal Boot the next morning, banging on the inside of the door with his fist. 'C'mon ... feet on the floor.' It was seven o'clock - where on earth had the night gone?

'Come on you dozy bloody lot, shake yourselves.' the corporal yelled, giving the door a good whack with his swagger stick again. 'You've ten minutes to get washed and dressed and 'fell in' outside. Breakfast's in a quarter of an hour, rest of yer kit and yer uniforms'll be issued straight after that so get on with it. Right?'

We groaned and did as we were told.

Getting our uniforms proved to be a more tedious task than either we or Corporal Boot had anticipated, for the quartermaster was out of stock of some sizes of boots, trousers, and jackets.

I got my boots and trousers alright, but I had to wait for a week for my size of jacket to come into stock. In the meantime, we had to wear whatever we'd been issued augmented by our own clothes, which made us look ridiculous of course, with some wearing sandals and others wearing boots, some in grey flannels and others in khaki uniform trousers. Most embarrassed were those, like me, who had to continue wearing their sports coats or polo-necked pullovers while the rest had khaki tunic tops. Fortunately, it was quite warm, and for most of the time we were in 'shirt sleeve order', i.e. no jackets, so our lack of uniformity was principally in respect of our lower bodies and feet. The fact we were dressed so idiotically was brought home to me one day when a burley, red faced and sweating, white overcalled female cook, leaned across the serving counter in the mess hall and offered me what looked to be a shovelful of Cottage Pie while asking … 'D'you fancy a bit, Alan?'

Everyone within earshot doubled up with laughter. I didn't, I coloured up with embarrassment. How the hell did she know my name? And then I realised why … I'd printed it and my identity number, Alan Grainger - 19025429 - in black laundry ink along one of the straps of my brand new white canvas braces, visible because I'd left my sports coat off and thereby introduced myself to anyone who could read. I was damned glad when the jackets arrived the next day.

Within a week we were a different outfit. We'd our full uniforms and were spitting and polishing with the best of them. Most of us had, at one time or another, been in either one of the cadet forces or the Boy Scouts, so we'd plenty of experience marching and parade ground drilling. It just needed those of us with experience to help those who'd none. Andy drew the short straw in this regard. The chap who slept under him, the guy from Eton College, apart from being unable to tell his left from his right, also found it difficult to make his left arm swing forward at the same time as his right leg. When he was 'marching' he'd swing left arm and leg forward at the same time which gave him a ridiculous gait similar to that of a waddling duck. He got it sorted out after a week of Andy's patient coaching but, as to knowing his right from his left ... well he never conquered that, and was always liable to turn left when the rest of us turned right.

Despite all our coaching, it was six weeks before we were allowed to take as much as a single step out of the barracks - before we looked like soldiers in other words. It had been tears and laughs all the way, but it had been time well spent too, and we'd finally been drilled into a disciplined and fairly smart bunch. Being confined to barracks had been awful, a terrible deprivation, and I began to see how demoralising being a prisoner might be.

We spent most of our off-duty time in the NAAFI (Navy, Army, and Air Force Institute) canteen, which was great because Becky was an amazingly good pianist. He could rattle off anything and, right from our first night, his talent paid off. He was playing in the main canteen when the roars of approval and applause, which rose as he'd finished a string of popular songs, brought one of the sergeants from their mess next door. He said Becky could have free beer all night if he went through to play for them.

'Alright,' Becky said. 'I will if I can bring my mates with me.'

They agreed, and every night for the next six weeks he banged away at the old upright in the sergeant's mess and Andy and I drank free beer.

As far as training was concerned, we were by then ready to fire rifles, throw grenades, and terrify the life out of the enemy with our bayonets. And we could quick march, slow march, and do miraculously dexterous things with our rifles. We were ready to move on and so we did, but not together, for at the end of our training we were split up. Andy and Becky and I had asked to be posted together to any non-infantry regiment (too much walking) - but it was not to be. In the end, and, after a forty eight hour leave during which I swaggered about Gerrard's Cross in my uniform hoping to be seen, I was sent to a heavy anti-aircraft (ack-ack) artillery training regiment, in Oswestry, up on the Welsh border; Andy went to the Royal Engineers depot at Gravesend; and Becky was posted to the Royal Corps of Signals at Catterick. We didn't see each other again until we were 'demobbed' nearly three years later.

Oswestry was hard going. The guns we were learning to use were huge, with a 16 foot long barrel and a bore of 3.7 inches. They could hurl a 25lb shell at an aircraft at a height of 32,000 feet, or at an enemy target on the ground 14 miles away. Despite their size we lugged them all over the Welsh mountains, setting them up and going through our firing drills. Winter was approaching by then, so we spent more and more time practicing within the confines of the camp on Park Hall Estate which, apart from being our base, was the HQ of Western Command - a great sprawling conglomeration of wooden huts called 'Spiders', clustered in sixes round central ablution blocks.

I had several short leaves during the time I was at Oswestry, thirty six and forty eight hour weekend passes; but the journey home was long, and the time there always seemed to be short. Even so, and despite the fact we didn't get a free travel warrant for 'a thirty six', I went home at every opportunity relying on help from my father to cover the fare. All except on one weekend that is …

Someone had told me the midnight train back to Oswestry from Paddington left from Platform One, at which there was no barrier, and that if you managed to avoid the ticket collector travelling on the train (and there wasn't always one on board) and you jumped off the train as it slowed when it approached the level crossing at Ruabon a short distance across the fields from our camp, you could avoid buying a ticket. Great, I thought, and the next time I got a weekend pass without a travel warrant I decided I'd try it.

I got caught of course ... Sod's Law. Everything had gone according to plan until I, like dozens of others, jumped out of the slowing train and rolled down the embankment south of Ruabon. At the bottom, was a cordon of military policemen! I knew I'd be for the high jump next day but, as it turned out, we got off with a caution and a week confined to barracks during which we had to report hourly to the duty sergeant, in the guardroom, in whatever clothes he'd specified on our previous visit.

It was coming up to Christmas when I was instructed to report to the War Office Selection Board at Chester for a three day interview to determine whether or not I was suitable to be sent to an officer training unit. I tried to find out what sort of things I might be asked but, in the end, I went there unprepared for the extraordinary tests to which I was put. In the main they were designed to measure initiative and leadership qualities, and they were dressed up in a series of outdoor exercises in which the ability of the candidates to deal with unexpected situations was carefully watched. In addition, all through the three days, not just when we were on an exercise, but even if we were simply sitting at a meal or chatting in the bar, we were constantly with the examiners and being assessed. It was a strange feeling, being 'spied on' and evaluated all the time.

I'd been back in Oswestry a week when the Colonel sent for me and told me I'd passed the selection board and been accepted for training at the Officer Cadet Training School in Aldershot. Four others from our unit had gone to Chester at the same time I did, two (of which I was one) had been selected, re-classified as 'Potential Officers', and given a white band to wear across our epaulettes to signify our new status. This understandably created a barrier between us and the rest of our hut-mates. It also made us the special target of the venom of Bombardier Mathews, a consummate bully, who used his modest rank to terrify us.

He was better known around the barracks as Bombardier 'Bastard' Maffews, a term he used himself, and he made life hell on earth for everyone arriving in Oswestry after their six weeks initial training in the General Service Corps (in Colchester in my case).

Without trying, he destroyed all the confidence we'd acquired under the tutelage of Corporal Boot who, we were beginning to recognize, was all bull, bluster, and heart. Bombardier Mathews was a totally different animal; his most renowned performance, repeated with every new intake, was to tell us that, when he was a boy, he'd had a set of toy soldiers. 'Toy soldiers my poor old muvver and farvver 'ad scrimped and saved to give me fer Christmas. I loved to play wiv those toy soldiers ... marching 'em up an' dahn ... up an' dahn. And then one day some rotten little bastard stole 'em. I cried, and I cried. 'Never mind son,' said my dear old muvver. 'maybe one day you'll get some more toy soldiers to play wif ... and by God she was right. Look what I've got ... I've got you lot, you miserable shower. Oh I'm going to get some fun out of you boys. What are *you* grinning at soldier? Wipe that smile of your face son, or I will ... you see if I don't. Nah ...let's try that all over again right? Open order ... march. Right dress ... c'mon, c'mon c'mon, I aven't got all day. Eyes ... front. Dis ... miss. Smartly now, smartly. No, no, don't run. C'mon get 'fell in' again, we'll have it right if we're here all night.'

He was an absolute nightmare, and I was glad when Oswestry was over and I was on the way to more exciting things, first at the Royal Artillery officer training unit at Mons and Deepcut Barracks, near Aldershot, and finally when I was posted to an active unit in Germany gaining my first command at the age of nineteen.

It's all so long ago now, and my life has changed direction so many times I can hardly believe how I spent some of my early adult years. Writing these few words has brought them all back into focus again. It's been like looking at myself through the wrong end of a telescope; a strange experience, showing me glimpses of how I was, and what I did, as a young man, when I was just setting out on a journey that I have yet to complete.

1983; The Joy in Innocence.

by

Natalie Cox

G ranny and Grandad are coming." The words sounded like a fluffy cake to me. I loved my granny and Grandad Mac. I was seven years old. My brother Derek was nine years old. I remember it was early summer, but it was warm and sunny and, although I was young, I realised sunny days were rare in the west of Ireland.

"When are they coming?" I shouted in glee.

"Saturday." my mum said.

I distinctly remember the feeling of excitement in my tummy. "How long are they staying?" I asked.

My mum smiled and said "Pack a bag, you are going on holidays with them." That sentence was a lot for my little brain to comprehend. I couldn't take it all in.

"Are you coming Mammy?" I asked.

"No Nat. Just you and Derek; and you are going for a whole week."

"Wow." I thought, happy but a little apprehensive - no Mammy!

I can't quite remember what day of the week she told Derek and I, but I do recall the remainder of the week felt incredibly long as we waited for Granny and Grandad's arrival. I probably spent the remainder of the week teasing my younger brothers and sisters; goading them about how much more loved I was, and how I was independent and ready for the adventure.

I packed and unpacked a rickety old suitcase possibly 20 times. I think I got some new dresses and new sandals - a big deal in the eighties in Roscommon. I felt like I was leaving forever with my comprehension of time being so disoriented. I remember my brother Derek packing at least 10 books and very few clothes. I teased him over and over again about this and he told me not to talk to him for the whole trip.

The night before Granny and Grandad arrived to pick us up, I couldn't sleep. A fusion of excitement and trepidation and a general disquiet prevented it. It still happens to me to this day. It didn't help that I knew Grandad had a new car, and that I was, let's say, car sick proficient! Mum, who at that time was known as 'Mammy' had warned me; "Don't get sick in the car". A warning that really came with no alternatives, albeit one I intended to do my best with.

Granny and Grandad arrived early on the Saturday morning. Driving from Dublin to Roscommon on roads before motorways. I remember watching their shiny white car driving in the gate, and it looked like a James Bond car to me. I have since established, through old photos, that it was in fact a Ford Fiesta.

I had dragged my old suitcase out and was waiting beside the car as it stopped, fully expecting someone would put my case in and we would turn around and leave. I had no interest in tea and conversations; my adventure was waiting and my serenity and innocence indifferent to all rules of normal behaviour.

What felt like time without end, finally ended, and we were on the road.

I can clearly remember the smell of that car like it was yesterday. It had soft seats and a wonderful smell which I now refer to as 'that new car smell'. It was so clean and polished I felt like a millionaire. To this day that smell brings me straight back to Granny and Grandad and that wonderful holiday.

I can't remember exactly how far we had travelled, but I distinctly recall that I started to feel travel sick.

My Grandfather was a Head Master, Master Mac. He loved to teach us Irish. I hated Irish; even as a seven-year-old I knew the language was not one where I was going to excel! This was now a problem for me, I was being asked to recite Irish while literally and ferociously trying to stop myself from throwing up in Grandad's new car.

Derek looked at me and, on seeing my particular shade of green, shouted, "She's going to get sick Grandad."

Grandad who was the most careful driver in Ireland had that car on a verge and me removed so quickly I wasn't sure what was happening.

The rest of the journey brought many stops and starts for 'air breaks'. When we got to what I now know is the Glenn of the Downs, I was mesmerised by the woods through which were driving. And I remember thinking the trees were so gigantic it was like I was entering Narnia.

My face was fixed firmly to the window throughout the journey and I truly felt as if I was part of a real voyage of adventure.

We arrived at our destination, *Brittas Bay* at some time later that evening.

Pulling up to our mobile home was magical. We explored every nook and cranny of it. We got hours of entertainment out of the bunk beds. Forts, castles, and caves were lived in through our imaginations that week.

Our week also took on a wonderful daily routine of breakfast, and what seemed like very long walks while reciting Irish and learning about the wildlife with Grandad. Then back to the mobile home for milk and scones before heading to the beach.

I recall Derek getting badly sunburned and refusing to stay out of the sun much to my grandmother's annoyance, I assume the pain was worth it.

Lunch was always at 12:30 and invariably consisted of egg sandwiches ... with an extra helping of sand!

Dinner was a barbeque every evening at 5:30. The time has stayed with me, for Grandad always insisted we had to be exactly on time.

At night time I can clearly recollect the

soothing sound of the sea, mixed with a little fear of being washed away, and then, reassured I wouldn't be, I gently fell asleep.

That week was full of joy and laughter and learning and kindness and, although it was only *Brittas Bay,* I know it firmly sowed the seed of adventure and travel in my heart.

It was the summer of 1983. Sadly, Grandad died the following year.

I am so grateful we had that wonderful week in Brittas together ... one in which I learned so much from him of the art of love of family, of respect of others, and of our friends and all around us. Magic.

"What'll you have?"

by

Will Durston

I enjoyed my time at Oundle. It was a large school, with around eight hundred boys, and one girl (the bursar's daughter, the poor soul). Like so many UK boarding schools, it dominates the town. Located in the east of Northamptonshire, Oundle is surrounded on three sides by the River Nene, and is a beautiful stone built market town that has served the surrounding valleys since Saxon times. The town centre has many fine stone houses over 300 years old, divided by narrow alleys and courtyards, above which the graceful spire of the parish church rises.

The school is over 450 years old, tracing its

history back to 1556. The school buildings are dispersed throughout the town, meaning that there was a lot of walking as part of my daily routine. During my tenure there were twelve boys' houses, with each house comprising sixty to seventy boys. I was in New House, which was right on the edge of the town, and a good ten to fifteen minute walk from the central Cloisters and all the classrooms. In spite of its name New House was actually the oldest house in the school and, as luck would have it, it was undergoing a multi-year modernisation programme during my five year tenure. This 'luck' meant that I would enjoy a completely refurbished living accommodation in my final two years; but it also meant I was living on a building site for the first three. I particularly remember the temporary dormitory in my third year, which was in a separate building with a woefully inadequate boiler and sash windows with gaps the size of your hand. In the winter we would regularly wake to find ice formed on the inside of the windows.

Discipline was tight at Oundle but as every schoolboy knows, rules are for breaking. I remember in my first year a particularly amusing prank in the summer term by the sixth formers of another house; it was the last day of term, and tradition had it that the whole school would attend chapel before heading off for the summer break. Oundle has an enormous chapel, and in my day it easily accommodated the entire school plus all the staff, with further room for those parents wishing to attend. Tradition had it that we would sing the school anthem 'Jerusalem' and for this reason alone it always had a good turnout of parents, keen to enjoy the belting-out of a classic by eight hundred male voices (most of them in key).

As we all filed into the chapel on my first ever experience of this end of term tradition, I heard a gentle sniggering (very much against the rules) which I put down to general excitement and end of term exuberance. I assumed the nearest school prefect would bring it under control but it grew louder, and then a voice shouted out "Look up!". At this point the entire congregation (perhaps not the staff) collapsed into laughter. Hanging from one of the ceiling cross-beams some fifty feet above us was a master's bicycle. There was no evidence of how this feat had been executed - no sign of ropes, ladders or aids of any sort. And it was hanging right in the middle of the chapel, to guarantee maximum impact. I later learnt that the bicycle belonged to a science teacher who also happened to be head of mountaineering. No doubt the perpetrators (who were never identified) had been personally coached by him at some point.

This prank became legendary and sparked a sense of competition amongst future school leavers for a similar end of academic year display of cunning and wit. I was impressed with the efforts of the leavers during my third year: the headmaster had a reputation for having very large feet, and so they made some huge cardboard footsteps (each one six feet long) and laid them out on the chapel lawn heading towards the chapel, up one side of the building, over the roof, and down the other side, before heading off towards the Cloisters. Technically harder than the suspended bicycle, and probably more dangerous. But the bicycle is my favourite.

When it came to testing the rules, I never managed anything quite so flash - and in any event I wasn't in the mountaineering club. In my third year, when we all turned sixteen, one of our year group in the house proposed a dawn drinking adventure - after all we were nearly at the legal drinking age. It was the summer term, exams had finished and it was that quiet period leading up to the end of term. Our first challenge was to get hold of some cider, the chosen tipple for the occasion. This was actually reasonably straightforward - we were all regular spenders at the local corner shop (the school tuck shop was a fifteen minute walk like everything else) and the shop owner was keen to retain our business, so he turned a blind eye. The illicit goods were then stored in our large wooden tuck boxes (always padlocked and, curiously in hindsight, a no-go area for prefects and masters during my entire school career) until the weekend. We all behaved impeccably in the days running up to the chosen Sunday morning, so as not to jeopardise the mission with any detentions or gatings. After the 10pm lights-out on Saturday night, there wasn't a whisper in the dorm - no banter, no pillow fights, nothing - it was straight to sleep. One of us was tasked with setting an alarm and at 4 am we quietly got dressed, crept downstairs, and out of the building. It was a half hour walk to a field we had chosen earlier in the week, containing a haystack. It was on a gentle hill with a clear view to the east, and we were blessed with a clear night sky. We made ourselves comfortable with armchairs and sofas formed out of hay bales, and we sat back and watched the dawn break over the Northamptonshire countryside, whilst downing copious quantities of cider.

Whilst we didn't get outrageously drunk, none of us remember much about the next few hours. Dawn had broken at about 5 am, and I think we crept back into the house at around 7 am.

Sunday mornings were always relaxed, there was no fixed routine as long as you made it to chapel on time. On that particular Sunday there was a choice of two services, 'early' or 'late'. Checks on who went to which service were lax, meaning you could play the system and not attend either. This wasn't a tactic to adopt regularly but there was no way any of us were putting ourselves in full visibility of anyone in authority. It was also an optional exeat day, which meant that after chapel you could spend the day at home if your parents were prepared to do the two school runs.

I only lived an hour away and my parents were always kind enough to give me a break from the routine. I remember feeling distinctly unwell; the car journey home was a particular challenge, my father drove a rather sporty Lancia Gamma and the country roads were twisty and undulating, but I managed to 'stay out of trouble' so to speak.

We approached my home village at about midday, and I was looking forward to a quiet afternoon in a dark room. But to my horror, just before we reached home, my father pulled into the local pub.

"You're sixteen now, I think it's time for a father and son pint. What would you like, beer or cider?"

"Not cider. Definitely not cider."

I haven't touched the stuff since.

What's good

about

The Good Old Days?

by

Miss Terrigest

The Good Old Days is a familiar phrase and it's a load of rubbish, or at least it is as far as my childhood was concerned.

I was born in the early thirties, and was just over three when World War II broke out. I can't remember any of the drama I now know was taking place as Germany, ignoring the world-wide condemnation of its actions, pressed ahead and invaded Poland. No, I can't recall anything of that and wouldn't have been able to comprehend it at the time even if I could. After all, at three years of age, I didn't know much beyond what was happening immediately in front of me.

Oddly enough, even at that tender age, from conversations I overheard, especially those that took place between my mother and father, I had a very strong sense of knowing things were different. Everyone kept saying they were … but different to what? I knew nothing of the way things had been before I was born; I only knew what was going on in front of my eyes there and then, and that, as far as I was concerned, meant being warm and free of hunger. I was. It's was only in my later years I began to appreciate how much my parents, and especially my mother, had to give up to ensure my brother and I were warm and well-fed during the first four or five years of the conflict. I wonder if a present-day child would be able to cope with the shortcomings that touched every part of our lives.

Take food for a start; it was rationed, and a single person would have to manage for a week on 6 ounces of meat, 2 ounces of butter, cheese, margarine, and tea, plus 3 pints of milk, 6 ounces of sugar, an egg, and ... for a treat ... once every eight weeks a one-pound jar of jam or marmalade. Even sweets were rationed with each person getting just 12 ounces every 4 weeks.

The rationing of clothing via a points system was the most peculiar issue. Each adult person was allowed sixty six points per year (children got twice that), and these could be spent to buy clothing, typical points per garment being: 11 points for a dress, two for a pair of stockings, and eight for a man's shirt or a pair of trousers. Women's shoes meant using five coupons, and men's footwear needed seven. When buying new clothes, the shopper had to hand over coupons with the appropriate number of points as well as the money. It was a weird system but it worked.

How would we manage on these miserable rations in this day and age though? How would we be able to cope with these limits on clothing, and others on the amount of bread and vegetables we needed to balance and bulk out our diet, and the miserable share of coal or oil for our fires or kitchen boilers. There was no petrol allowed for anyone other than a few people in essential occupations like doctors, and there was no fruit available bar that grown locally in people's garden or on allotments made in public parks and sports fields.

I can't remember seeing an orange, a banana, or a grape, from when I was around four until I was well over eight.

To back up the miserable portions we were able to purchase in the local shops, most people grew their own vegetables and fruit and kept a few hens.

I am utterly astonished at the way my mother, and to a lesser extent my father, contrived to let me believe this was all quite normal. I cannot recall ever thinking things had ever been any other way until I was getting on for nine or ten, and then the true picture began to emerge; then I began to see how things had once been and how they would be again when the war was over. It was a strange enlightening; one quite hard to grasp and, as the real picture started to emerge, I began to see I would never be able to repay my parents for sacrificing their entitlements to keep my brother and I safe, happy, and warm, until the better days came.

And they did … but only after the Good Old Days had been put to bed, for there's nothing good about the good old days.

One of The Boys

By

Eleanor Bourke

I had a great childhood - full of fun, adventures and freedom.

There was my brother, who was three years older than I was. There then followed two younger sisters, the youngest being a baby when I was eight years old.

My brother was the instigator and trouble shooter. He had the ideas, and I followed and joined in everything, wanting to be part of the boys' club and being with the boys.

We were privileged to have grown up in a rambling house with lots of space away from our parents. They never really knew what we were doing. At dinner one night, years after, when we were in our 30s, we told them our stories and what we had been up to when we were kids. They were horrified and amused; laughing and frowning at the same time. Mind you, we never told them about the most horrific of the antics in which we had been engaged.

Some recollections then …..

My brother, with four of his friends, had the White Hood Club (they had made white hoods cut from sheets to go over their heads and cut slits in them for their eyes). They used to meet in one end of the house in a room with no windows, so candles had to be lit, and they'd sit round a table plotting the devilment they intended to get up to.

I never knew what it was going to be, but definitively mischief was on the agenda! Anyhow I was desperate to be part of the club. They were all boys and 11/12 years of age. They allowed me to bring them Mi-wadi or tea and biscuits and wait on them! In order to *join* the club however, I had to have a little cross cut into my arm with a knife. They all sniggered when I held out my arm and my brother got his pen knife out! I was the guinea pig, none of them had this done to them. It went on from there ... climbing to the top of very tall trees to see how high I could climb and being left up there when I couldn't get down without help as I felt dizzy due to the height. They would all laugh below. But I would eventually beat the fear and make it down still wanting to be approved by the boys' club.

Another recollection was 'dare deviling' – we were always on our bikes and so we used to cycle, one by one, as fast as we could down the avenue and go straight out our gate onto the Glenageary Road without stopping – the idea being to *nearly* hit a car. We didn't think about being killed; we were invincible! And, in those days of course, there were few cars on the road. The driver of the car would jam on his brakes in fright when he saw us and then, in anger, turn the car around and chase after us … this was the adrenalin rush!

We would take off down Albert Road at speed and then, just before the driver caught up with us, we would cycle off into 'the metals', laughing our heads off for the car could not follow us through there and we would be free of the chase!

Once I was caught by a driver and I thought I was really going to 'get it', after being dragged back to my parents. But this man was so lovely – he made me sit down on the pavement and patiently explained to me exactly the harm I could cause to myself and the driver of the car involved. He asked me if, in the event he had run me down, how did I think *he* would feel trying to explain to my parents what had happened to their lovely daughter. And he also asked if had had given any thought to the trauma *he'd* have experienced and the fear he suffer if the accident was deemed to be his fault when, in truth, it was mine.

He asked me why was I doing it too? I

couldn't explain, except to say it was the most exhilarating fun I'd ever had. He made me feel so guilty ... but in a lovely kind way. I took heed and never did it again.

Another memory my brother devised was a trick with a parcel attached to fishing gut.

There was an old shed behind the wall in a field across the road from us.

Three of four of us would crouch on the roof of the shed, which was lower than the wall, so we could not be seen from the road.

My brother used to pack a box with mud and stones and then expertly wrapped it in brown paper with a postage stamp and a name and address on it. This parcel would be left lying on the pavement as if it had been dropped by someone. He would have tied a piece of fishing gut around the package and he, or one of his friends, would have the other end of the gut in his hand while we all crouched behind the wall.

A passer-by would walk by, take a look, walk on, hesitate, and then walk back not sure whether to pick the parcel up or not. Inevitably they would look at it for a moment and then take it up, read the address (which would be one on Glenageary Road) ... and would be thinking, we assumed, that they ought to drop the parcel off at the address as they were walking by, saying someone must have dropped it. Just as they would be about to walk off with the parcel, my brother would pull the fishing gut and the parcel would fly out of the hands of whoever had picked it up who then usually jumped back in bewilderment and fright as peals of laughter came from behind the wall.

Some of the people we 'caught' had a good sense of humour and laughed with us, but others were very cross and gave out! It worked every time, and we spent hours every other day in summer with this trick. I remember so well what great entertainment it was for us.

In those days my father had accounts in a lot of the local stores. One was the hardware store in Dun Laoghaire. My brother having devised from his

science books how to make copper bombs sent me
off to the hardware store on my bicycle to get copper
pipes and sodium chloride. I can't remember if
anything else was needed. Anyway, a plan was made
that I would go and ask for the chemicals that he'd
written down on a list he gave me on one day, and
then the copper piping on another day, so as not to
raise suspicion. If asked, I would always say to the
man behind the counter that my father had sent me to
do the errand for him. Then followed the great
excitement as I watched my brother and his friends
stuffing the copper pipes with the chemicals. They
were scientific experiments, my brother told us, as
we sat around a fire we had made, eating completely
blackened potatoes we had cooked on the fire … and
baked beans.

Then the copper bomb was placed in the
wooded area of the garden alongside the avenue, and
a trail of the chemicals led back from the stuffed pipe
up to where we were. This was then lit and we would
crouch behind a tree trunk and wait for the fire trail

to arrive at the bomb which would then explode, thrilling us as our laughter rang out.

We were soon stopped though, as the hardware store checked with my father to see if he had really ordered the bomb materials.

Luckily for me, I became passionate about riding ponies and then horses around this time, so my tom boy days ended soon after … but the fond memories always make me smile.

A Brush with The Law.

by

Derek Phillips

"Congratulations you are now the proud owner of your new Ford Anglia ...."

I wasn't proud, I was nervous and excited, as I read the manual, realising that, in a few hours, I would be driving an 18 year old car home from Braemor Road at four in the morning, a time when the guards, and everyone else including my parents, would be asleep in their beds, and have no idea what Grant and I would be up to.

I was thirteen years old at the time, and had in my pocket the keys to the 1963 Ford Anglia we had jointly purchased.

It was mid-term break and we'd worked a full week in H Williams supermarket in the Rathfarnham Shopping Centre. We had earned the vast sum of 80 pounds between us. It was all the money we had, and we had handed it over to an elderly neighbour, Mrs Findlay who had just moved out of her house and into an apartment when progressive arthritis left her unable to drive. We told her 'an older friend' would pick it up late that evening and the car would be a restoration project until we were the legal age to drive.

I had never driven a car on the road before, but my father let me change the gears for him and, later, he would let me go as far as actually starting the engine. Unbeknown to him though, I would move the car up and down the driveway possibly five feet at a time. Not much, but enough to know the basic operation of the clutch and the brakes. I loved cars and I was in a hurry to get driving.

Our adventure began at about 4.00 a.m., sneaking out in our socks so as not to wake anyone.

Mrs Findlay's apartment was about a mile away and we ran excitedly most of that way. It was still dark, and would be so for a couple of hours; we had a mission ahead of us.

Into the apartment carpark, and in front of us sat what was to be our pride and joy. It hadn't been driven or started in months. The black paintwork had faded badly, but I knew T-Cut and elbow grease would sort that out. The car only had 56,000 miles on its clock, not much for one that was 18 years old.

Opening the creaking doors, we climbed into the old vehicle and, with hands trembling, savoured the moment we had been dreaming about for months. This was it … now things were about to happen.

I put the key in to the ignition, pulled the choke out half way and shoved the gear stick into neutral. "Here we go." I said, as I turned the ignition key to position 1 and a light came on … exciting!

I held my breath then turned the key to position 2, but nothing happened.

I turned the key again, and got a little feeble click from the starter motor.

I looked at Grant,

"Let me try." he said.

I shook my head and prayed I hadn't been doing something wrong; all I was trying to do was start the thing, was I now going to be robbed of driving it?

"It's alright, I'll try again." I muttered, closing my eyes and willing the engine to fire.

Still nothing … only another feeble click.

We had a flat battery.

"So what?" I said to Grant, "Nothing's going to stop a couple of guys like us … smart kids who have grown up in the 70's."

A push start, that would solve it; it solved every car ailment in our world.

Braemar road hill was right beside us.

Perfect!

I had done this manoeuvre with my father and siblings so many times in the early 70's. It was basically how each day would begin, by push-starting the family Volkswagen Beetle. Three kids doing so from the back with my father, standing beside the open driver's door and shoving from the side.

Once the car had decent momentum he would hop into the driver's seat, quickly press in the clutch, bang the gear lever into second then, as he slowly let the clutch again, the car would bunny-hop as it spluttered into life with the familiar "phut phut" sound of the VW Beetle engine

It was a two-door car, the passenger door didn't open, so his next trick was to keep revving the engine while tilting his seat forward enough to let us kids climb behind him and into the back seat. I remember at the time thinking there was nothing unusual for him to be squeezed up against the steering wheel face pressed against the window while we jumped in with the car still in motion. Now it plays back in my mind like a scene from The Simpsons!

I could only have been six or so at the time I

reckon, and we had that car a good number of years, but the black on red registration <u>312 AZJ</u>, remains etched in my memory.

Grant and I were by then pushing the car out of the car park and onto the other side of the road to the top of the Braemar road hill.

It was more arduous than we'd thought and, as I considered myself the "experienced driver", I pushed from the front, as had my Dad, fully ready to jump into the driver's seat. We had earlier argued who would drive the car home. I insisted I would do it, having had more experience than Grant. After all, I had actually started an engine … and with a key!!!

Once on the hill, the car started to pick up momentum, I jumped into the driver's seat, ignition on, clutch in, but it would not go into second gear no matter what I did.

"Put it into gear, you twit." roared Grant.

"I can't; it won't go in" I roared back.

"Push in the clutch for Goodness's sake".

"I *am* pushing it in. But it still won't go, and we're running out of hill!"

I stopped the car, slamming on the brakes, hoping that, once stationery, the car would slip easily into the chosen gear.

"Strange." I thought, when it didn't.

We were beginning to panic, not wanting to draw attention to ourselves in the black of the night. We just wanted to get the car going and get the hell out of there.

We tried again, but once more the car would not go into gear and Grant, exhausted from pushing, was getting desperate and began to lag behind.

I rammed the lever into first gear as hard as I could. To my astonishment there was an awful almighty crunch, and then a splutter, a bunny hop, and the engine fired into life ... lurching the car forward at speed.

"Wow, I didn't expect that." I said, quickly depressing the clutch and footbrake until the car slowed. And then, pulling the hand brake as hard as I could, I finally brought the car to a halt.

At the same time, I had somehow managed to rev up the engine to keep it going.

I looked all around me. There was a haze of blue exhaust smoke everywhere.

Grant, who'd caught me up by then, couldn't believe it; but he climbed in anyway, relieved when I revved the engine and slowly let out the clutch.

"Janey! We're nearly at the bottom of the hill." he panted, "Imagine having to push it all the way back home to Rathfarnham … and switch on the God-dammed lights for Goodness's sake."

We were by then doing 10 miles per hour and I changed into second gear. Not the smoothest of gear changes but, thankfully, it changed. We're going twenty five miles an hour now … and we're into third gear.

"Push in the choke Derek"

"That's it …. fantastic, she's running like a beauty."

We pulled up to the red traffic lights, breathed

a sigh of relief, shook hands ... and laughed.

The engine was by then ticking over quite happily.

"Why d'you think it wouldn't go into gear?" Grant asked.

"I dunno." I replied, "but it seems grand now."

Later, I'd learn that the clutch had temporarily seized as a result of the car having been sitting in Mrs Findlay's garage, unused, for months. Luckily, everything freed up when the engine finally started.

We turned the corner, then up Rathfarnham Road and onto Rathfarnham Park, where we drove a couple of times around the block, then up Ballytore Road and back via Crannagh Road. This was a true adventure, we thought.

I was by then pretty confident and having the time of my life.

"Let's go further," I said, "what about the Pine Forest, we haven't been up there in a while?"

"Yeah ... why not?"

Back onto the main Rathfarnham Road and approaching the Yellow House pub, we realised the Garda station was only around the corner, so we took it carefully, not wanting to attract attention. Slowly we made our way past the Tuning Fork Pub and up the winding road and hills that lead to the Pine Forest.

Accelerator to the floor by then, but this old lady wasn't going fast, the hills got steeper and, though the engine laboured a lot, we finally got to the top of the Mountain where you could see the spectacular sight of Dublin city lights glowing in the distance. Not a soul was around and we cautiously decided we better make our way back while it was still dark.

Driving down the mountain was a different experience, with the car easily gaining speeds of which neither the car or I were capable of controlling!

A couple of times I entered a bend far too fast and the car shot onto the wrong side of the road.

Grant was terrified; yelling at me to slow down. But with useless brakes and soft tyres it was an act of God that we got back in one piece.

Nevertheless, we were hooked, and we took the car for one last spin around the block this time with Grant at the wheel, determined to drive faster than I had. I held onto the bottom of the seat as the car slid around the corner, engine screaming and tyres squealing. We thought we were better than Starsky and Hutch ... albeit in a very uncool car.

We parked it just around the corner, well out of sight of both our parents' houses and, sneaking into the kitchen, we got breakfast going while we talked in excited tones that awakened Grant's twin sister.

She couldn't believe we had bought Mrs Findlay's car and begged us to bring her for a spin. We couldn't resist, and immediately abandoned our half eaten breakfast to bring her for a quick turn around the block. The car had to be push-started again, so Grant and his sister, still in her pyjamas, started to get it moving.

I was just about to climb in, when a Blue

squad car with two uniformed Guards came around the corner and stopped beside us, lights flashing.

Grant turned white and sat down thinking he was going to faint. The high of the previous exhilarating hours quickly evaporated to one of dreaded fear, anxiety, and a rapid realisation of all the trouble we were in: the tyres had insufficient tread and were not fully inflated, there were no current tax or insurance discs showing, and, even more serious, neither of us had a driving licence or was old enough to apply for one.

On top of that, there're was the risk of them adding 'dangerous driving'. Were we going to be arrested and put in prison? Worse … would they wake up our parents and tell them what we'd been doing? They'd have a fit!

"So what are ye lads up to?" the first Guard asked, while the second Guard took out his notebook to write down our details.

"Names?"

We mumbled an answer

"Address?"

This time we whispered; it was almost as if we thought our parents were listening.

"Age?"

"Thirteen."

"Thirteen? ... *Thirteen*!"

The Guards didn't know what to make of it. We told them we had just bought the car as part of a school project and were pushing it home. Grant's sister, we told them, had come out to help us for the last bit of the journey as we were exhausted.

"Are you sure none of you were driving the vehicle?" the Guard asked, looking at us suspiciously as he kicked the tyre he was standing beside.

"No." I muttered, manufacturing a feeble grin in the hope it might gain his sympathy.

I don't think it did, for I could see the disbelief in his face.

"Sure we don't even know how to drive." I said, trying again to make light of our plight

"Really? That's different to what I heard." the

Guard replied. "We've had a number of phone calls from people in this area saying that two young hooligans have been seen driving around the area at high speed in a stolen car.

"That's not us." I said, indignantly. "Sure the car doesn't even go … try it yourself."

The Guard held out his hand. "Key!"

I smiled again and, trembling, gave it to him. I must have been one of the very few people in history who hoped their car wouldn't start. Not right then anyway.

Thankfully the battery was lifeless, and the Guard didn't realise the engine was still warm so, lucky for us, and with nothing concrete to charge us with, they let us off with a firm warning.

We couldn't believe our luck.

And did it stop us driving?

No, it did not; we were only just beginning!

Printed in Great Britain
by Amazon